21

D0832753

# THE
# WINTER'S TALE.

EDITED BY

## C. H. HERFORD, Litt. D., F.B.A.

**BLACKIE & SON LIMITED**
LONDON AND GLASGOW

BLACKIE & SON LIMITED
 *5 Fitzhardinge Street*
 *London, W.1*
 *17 Stanhope Street, Glasgow*
BLACKIE & SON (INDIA) LIMITED
 *103/5 Fort Street, Bombay*

*Printed in Great Britain by Blackie & Son, Ltd., Glasgow*

# GENERAL PREFACE

In the WARWICK SHAKESPEARE an attempt is made to present the greater plays of the dramatist in their literary aspect, and not merely as material for the study of philology or grammar. Criticism purely verbal and textual has only been included to such an extent as may serve to help the student in his appreciation of the essential poetry. Questions of date and literary history have been fully dealt with in the Introductions, but the larger space has been devoted to the interpretative rather than the matter-of-fact order of scholarship. Æsthetic judgments are never final, but the Editors have attempted to suggest points of view from which the analysis of dramatic motive and dramatic character may be profitably undertaken. In the Notes likewise, while it is hoped that all unfamiliar expressions and allusions have been adequately explained, yet it has been thought even more important to consider the dramatic value of each scene, and the part which it plays in relation to the whole. These general principles are common to the whole series; in detail each Editor is alone responsible for the plays entrusted to him.

Every volume of the series has been provided with a Glossary, an Essay upon Metre, and an Index;

and Appendices have been added upon points or special interest which could not conveniently be treated in the Introduction or the Notes.

By the systematic arrangement of the introductory matter, and by close attention to typographical details, every effort has been made to provide an edition that will prove convenient in use.

In the present book some lines in different portions of the text are omitted.

# CONTENTS

# THE WARWICK SHAKESPEARE. General editor, Professor C. H. HERFORD, Litt.D., F.B.A.

| Play | Edited by |
|---|---|
| ANTONY AND CLEOPATRA. | A. E. Morgan, M.A., and W. Sherard Vines, M.A. |
| As You Like It. | J. C. Smith, M.A., B.A. |
| CORIOLANUS. | Sir Edmund K. Chambers, K.B.E., C.B., M.A., D.Litt. |
| CYMBELINE. | A. J. Wyatt, M.A. |
| HAMLET. | Sir Edmund K. Chambers. |
| HENRY THE FOURTH—Part I. | F. W. Moorman, B.A., Ph.D. |
| HENRY THE FOURTH—Part II. | C. H. Herford, Litt.D., F.B.A. |
| HENRY THE FIFTH. | G. C. Moore Smith, D.Litt., Ph.D., LL.D. |
| JULIUS CÆSAR. | Arthur D. Innes, M.A. |
| KING JOHN. | G. C. Moore Smith. |
| KING LEAR. | D. Nichol Smith. |
| LOVE'S LABOUR'S LOST. | A. E. Morgan, M.A., and W. Sherard Vines, M.A. |
| MACBETH. | Sir Edmund K. Chambers. |
| THE MERCHANT OF VENICE. | H. L. Withers. |
| A MIDSUMMER-NIGHT'S DREAM. | Sir Edmund K. Chambers. |
| MUCH ADO ABOUT NOTHING. | J. C. Smith, M.A., B.A. |
| OTHELLO. | C. H. Herford, Litt.D., F.B.A. |
| RICHARD THE SECOND. | C. H. Herford. |
| RICHARD THE THIRD. | Sir George Macdonald, K.C.B., D.Litt., LL.D. |
| ROMEO AND JULIET. | J. E. Crofts, B.Litt. |
| THE TEMPEST. | F. S. Boas, M.A., LL.D. |
| TROILUS AND CRESSIDA. | Bonamy Dobrée, O.B.E., M.A. |
| TWELFTH NIGHT. | Arthur D. Innes, M.A. |
| THE WINTER'S TALE. | C. H. Herford. |

# INTRODUCTION

## SUMMARY

§ 1. The date and source of the play. Greene's *Pandosto*. The Greek romance writers.

§ 2. The plot of Greene's romance.

§ 3. Shakespeare's treatment of romance in *As You Like It* and in *The Winter's Tale*.

§ 4. The characteristics of Shakespeare's later plays; his treatment of pastoralism in *The Winter's Tale*.

§ 5. The changes which Shakespeare made in Greene's story.

§ 6. The pastoral scene. *Pandosto* transformed beyond recognition into beautiful poetry and tense drama.

§ 7. The recognition scene contrasted with *Cymbeline* and other plays.

§ 8. The natural magic of the end of the play. *The Winter's Tale* shows a change, not merely in theatrical fashion, but in Shakespeare. The unequalled harmony of the close.

§ 1. *The Winter's Tale*, it is universally agreed, was one of the latest of Shakespeare's plays. *The Tempest* and *Cymbeline* may be a little earlier or a little later; Shakespeare's portion of *Henry VIII* was certainly performed later (June, 1613), and was probably written not much earlier than this date; no other of his plays comes into question. The three "comedies" named belong to the class which the Elizabethans, after the Italians, called Tragi-comedy, and to the particular class of them which have been known in England latterly as "Romances", marked by separation and reunion of kinsfolk, and a deliberately unreal use of space and time. The three plays have also in common a heightened degree of the involved and elliptical style which first emerges in *Macbeth*, as well as a bold and often exceedingly beautiful subordination of the line to the sentence or the paragraph in verse-rhythm, which is in *Macbeth* as yet only distantly approached.

*The Winter's Tale* was certainly composed before 15th May, 1611, when Simon Forman, a London astrologer, saw it performed at the Globe; describing the play afterwards, unmistakably, in his rather perfunctory "Notes". It was performed on the following 5th November at Whitehall. There is every reason to think that it was recent, if not new, when Forman saw it, and that it still wore the glamour of a fresh success on the popular stage when played, as plays with that recommendation commonly were, at Court. That it gave high satisfaction there is clear from the fact that it was among the plays chosen for performance at the wedding festivities of the Princess Elizabeth in 1613. A year later its popularity (like that of *The Tempest*) drew a surly tribute from Ben Jonson when he made "the author" in the Induction to *Bartholo-mew Fair* protest in the name of realism and "nature" against "tales, tempests, and such like drolleries". Some of "the tale's" offences against "nature", in particular the "sea-coast of Bohemia", remained,[1] and even now remain, a traditional jest against the play; but did not affect its popularity. It was twice again performed at Court (in 1623 and 1633) before the Civil War.

This geographical offence did not, however, originate with Shakespeare. It was taken over, together with the substance of the plot, from the prose romance of *Pandosto: The Triumph of Time*, written by his old rival, Robert Greene (d. 1592), and first published in 1588. It was re-issued with the fresh title (from its hero and heroine, the counterparts of Florizel and Perdita) *The Hystorie of Doras-tus and Fawnia*, already used as running title in the first edition in 1607; but Shakespeare appears to have used the first edition only. Greene was not a good novelist nor a great writer. But in this romance he wove together in a loose context several types of subject-matter which were then highly popular in England, and held at least some germs

[1] It was sarcastically referred to again by Jonson in his "Conversations" with Drummond in 1619, and by Taylor, the water poet, in 1630.

of lasting interest.[1]  Such were, in particular: the innocent wife slandered by a jealous husband, and finally vindicated, but too late to save her life; the child sent adrift on the sea and cast up on a distant shore; the unknown princess brought up as a shepherdess, and later wooed in her homely Arcadia by a prince.  All these motives owed their Elizabethan popularity primarily to one or other of three famous Greek romances of the early Christian era, all familiar in translation to the England of Greene.  These were (1) *Theagenes and Chariclea* of Heliodorus (*c.* A.D. 250-300); (2) *Clitophon and Leucippe*, by Achilles Tatius (A.D. 400–500); (3) *Daphnis and Chloe*, by Longus (? A.D. 200).[2]  We are not here concerned directly with the origins of Greene's romance.  It will therefore suffice to say that the trial of the queen for unchastity and her vindication by the pronouncement of an oracle, together with the exposure and discovery of the child, and the later adventures and shipwreck of the two lovers, are modelled upon Heliodorian situations; while the upbringing of the child among shepherds is more closely borrowed from Longus.  From Achilles Tatius, a grosser writer than either of the others, he took the repulsive incident of the king making violent love to his own (unknown) daughter.  There is some evidence that Shakespeare consulted Longus (no doubt in Day's English version, 1587) for himself, since he has, as will be seen below, some details not found in Greene.

§ 2. The plot of Greene's romance is briefly this.  We dwell only on the points in which Shakespeare has diverged from this his principal source.

(1) Pandosto, king of Bohemia, suspects his queen, Bellaria, and their guest Egistus, king of Sicily, of a guilty intrigue.  The suspicion is unfounded; but they are devotedly attached, and the queen allows herself imprudent (though innocent) freedoms, "oftentimes coming herself

---

[1] It was, in fact, repeatedly translated, in the early seventeenth century, in France and Holland.

[2] S. L. Wolff, *The Greek Romances in Elizabethan Prose Fiction*, to which the following details are due.

into his bed-chamber, to see that nothing should be amiss to mislike him".

(2) Pandosto, after long consideration, resolves to end this, and instructs his cupbearer, Franion, to poison Egistus. Franion, however, gives him warning, and Egistus makes good his escape. Pandosto, infuriated, throws his wife into prison. There she bears a child, which, assuming it not to be his own, Pandosto orders to be cast adrift in an open boat, "having neither sail nor rudder to guide it, . . . and so to be carried into the midst of the sea, and there left to the wind and wave as the destinies please to appoint". The sentence is reluctantly carried out, the child being wrapped in a scarlet mantle, with a gold chain about its neck.

(3) The queen herself is arraigned for trial, on the double charge of adultery and of conspiring against her husband's life. The jury acquit her, but Pandosto refuses to abide by their verdict. Bellaria thereupon entreats her husband to ask the "oracle of Apollo" in "the Isle of Delphos" to decide. He reluctantly consents, and his messengers return with an unequivocal declaration from the god to the effect that "Bellaria is chaste: Egistus blameless: Franion a true subject: Pandosto treacherous: his babe an innocent: and the king shall live without an heir if that which is lost be not found". Upon this, Pandosto surrenders without reserve and begs forgiveness of his wife. But it is too late. News is brought of the death of the young prince Garintes, and the queen dies under the double shock. The king swoons, and recovering after three days, builds a monumental tomb to his wife and son.

(4) The romance now takes up the story of the queen's infant daughter, Fawnia, cast adrift at sea. Since it is guided only by "wind and wave", it is only by "Fortune" (as we say, by chance) that it is cast ashore on the coast of Sicily, the country of Egistus. A shepherd, Porrus, seeking a strayed sheep on the shore, finds the child, in its scarlet mantle and gold chain, and carries her home to his wife Mopsa. Fawnia is brought up in the shep-

herd's cottage as their daughter. Sixteen years pass, and this shepherd girl has become so fair that "she seemed to be the goddess Flora herself for beauty". At a festive meeting of rustic folks she is seen by Dorastus, son of Egistus, and they mutually fall in love. Dorastus, aware that he will not be allowed to marry her, proposes to elope with her, and with the help of his servant Capnio, prepares a ship, on which they secretly embark. But Porrus has in the meantime, in alarm, decided to disclose to Egistus what he knows of Fawnia, and the signs of her high birth. He is intercepted, however, by Capnio, and compelled to join the lovers in their flight.

(5) After a stormy voyage, the fugitives safely land on the "coast of Bohemia", and proceed to appear before the king. Pandosto suspects their feigned account of themselves, arrests Dorastus, and makes bold advances to his unrecognized daughter, which she firmly repels. In the meantime, Egistus, having learned of the lovers' plight, sends envoys to Pandosto's court in pursuit. Pandosto, enraged, summons Fawnia, Capnio, and Porrus before him, and condemns them all to death. Then at last Porrus, producing Fawnia's mantle and chain, reveals her identity, a joyful recognition ensues, and the Bohemian people celebrate the recovery of the long lost princess; while Pandosto, in remorse for his two-fold sin of treachery to his friend, and unnatural love, ends his life.

§ 3. Such was the romance which Shakespeare took in hand as material for the present play. He had once before, some ten years earlier, turned a popular romance to account in the same way, the principal story of *As You Like It* being drawn from the *Rosalynd* of Thomas Lodge. The two romances are composed of much the same ingredients—a serious story, threatening at times a tragic issue, and an amusing entanglement of lovers in pastoral and woodland scenery, leading to final reunion and recognition. The differences between them are such as we may expect in two works of the same *genre*, written in compliance with the same literary fashion, by men not very

unequal in talent or unlike in experience.    Far deeper
and more significant are the divergences between the two
comedies.   Some of these may be put down to Shakespeare's
deliberate compliance with the swiftly changing modes of
the Elizabethan stage during that momentous first decade
of the seventeenth century, and in particular with the
brilliant and fascinating new type of tragi-comedy which
was introduced about 1605 by the young John Fletcher.
It has been made probable by Prof. A. Thorndike[1] that
this Fletcherian type, with its serious and pathetic main
plot, its sudden turns and surprises of fortune, and its
deliberately unreal handling of place and time, attracted
the later Shakespeare, and has left its impress on the three
" Romances " of which *The Winter's Tale* was one.    We
may perhaps explain in this way the immensely increased
importance, in our play, of the serious story.    Frederick
and Oliver in *As You Like It* are as tyrannical, and as
headstrong in their tyranny, as Leontes.    But their harsh-
ness to Rosalind and Orlando is little more than a theatrical
device to get the lovers into Arden and set on foot the
joyous imbroglios which are our real concern.    *As You
Like It*, again, contains some surprising turns of fortune,
such as the sudden conversion of the two tyrants at the
close.    But these are the kind of laxity which Shakespeare permitted himself often enough in the comedies
when anxious, as Johnson said, " to finish his play ".    They
are quite distinct from the sharp revulsions which mark
throughout its course *The Winter's Tale* and *Cymbeline.*
The great closing scene of the latter play is a superb
example of what this technique could effect in the hands
of Shakespeare.    And Shakespeare, it is to be noted, does
not merely take over the romantic revulsions and incoher-
ences which he found in Greene ; he deliberately heightens
or adds to them.    Thus Pandosto's jealousy is excusable ;
that of Leontes fatuous ; and besides taking over Bohemia's
sea-coast from Greene, he introduces the new incoherence
of a Julio Romano contemporary with the Oracle of Delphi.

---

[1] *The Influence of Beaumont and Fletcher upon Shakespeare.*

§ 4. But some of the differences which strike every reader in comparing *The Winter's Tale* with *As You Like It* cannot be explained by changes in dramatic fashion. Ten years of intense creative energy may or may not have diminished Shakespeare's creative power; but they had modified some of the habits of his mind. His thinking had grown more complex without growing less swift; his writing, in consequence, often at once involved and elliptical. His verse-music had lost nothing of its transcendent beauty, but it moved more readily now in the graver than in the lighter keys, and its movement tended habitually rather to a large undulation than to the swift and agile phrase. His humour was both less spontaneous and (whatever the explanation) less akin to, less easily made a vehicle for, his poetry. Nowhere in these three plays do we hear the brilliant laughter of the middle comedies. Autolycus is pedestrian compared with Touchstone, not to speak of the Fool in *Lear*, the last of Shakespeare's poetic humorists (however much he be beside). His joy in womanhood was as profound and as delicate as ever; but it now attached itself to a somewhat altered ideal of woman. His young women have a natural loveliness of soul unsurpassed in literature; his matrons, like Hermione and Catherine in *Henry VIII*, an equally unsurpassed nobility and dignity; but the brilliant challenging wit of Rosalind and Beatrice is no longer heard. Rosalind and Portia don masculine dress as much for the jest's sake as for the need; Imogen, with a broken heart, solely as protection for her honour, which is now all that she cares for in life.

Somewhat similar, but subtler, is the difference between Rosalind and Perdita. Each is the central figure in a pastoral scene; and each provides in some sort a clue to Shakespeare's attitude, at these different dates, towards the literary fashion of Pastoralism, so captivating to many illustrious Elizabethan minds. It would not be strange if Shakespeare had for a while undergone the enchantment of that brilliant Arcadian world in which Spenser and Sidney had lingered with so much apparent content.

But the *Shepherd's Calendar* was soon superseded by the more strenuous and sincere symbolism of the *Faery Queene*, and the *Arcadia* by the more masculine passion of the sonnets to Stella. There is no sign that Shakespeare's imagination was at any time thus captured by Pastoralism. In *As You Like It*, certainly, where he was refashioning for his purpose a pastoral romance, he makes undisguised fun of this literary fashion. Literary Arcadia is admitted, it is true, into his greenwood Arden, but only to be gaily mocked in the persons of Silvius and Phœbe—samples of the amorous swains and coy maids who exchanged euphuistic altercations in the romances—and ironically confronted, in William and Audrey, with the homely creatures of the actual shepherd world. And into this half-real, half-fantastic Arden breaks the splendid apparition of Rosalind, at once a sportive Arcadian and a witty and passionate woman, whose intense poetic veracity makes both literary Pastoralism and rustic actuality insignificant.

In *The Winter's Tale* the handling is perceptibly different. Literary Pastoralism is no longer ridiculed, though Shakespeare had in Greene's romance a conspicuous example of it before his eyes. Phœbe and Silvius have no counterpart whatever here. William and Audrey, on the contrary, are multiplied. It is now, indeed, the actual shepherd world which dominates the picture. The old shepherd, and the farm girls, Mopsa and Dorcas, have come straight, one may guess, from the Stratford countryside to which Shakespeare had by now, it is probable, retired. Autolycus, too, "littered under Mercury" though he professed to be, is a true rogue-pedlar of the English lanes and homesteads. But Perdita belongs, like Rosalind, to another world, and hers is the veracity of poetry, not of actuality. Only, while Rosalind is a brilliant intruder in the pastoral scene, Perdita has grown up in it, and in her own belief belongs to it; and only unconscious pressure of her inherited nature has given her simplicity that magical appeal which calls forth Polixenes's involuntary tribute:

> Nothing she does or seems
> But smacks of something greater than herself,
> Too noble for this place.

§ 5. We must now turn to describe more in detail the changes introduced by Shakespeare in the process of transforming the romance into the play. To begin with the title. He did not call the play *Leontes*, or *Florizel and Perdita*, but *The Winter's Tale*—thus forestalling rationalist cavil at the outset by a frank disclaimer of actuality and even coherence. It was to be such stuff as old women tell children by the fireside. We are not, of course, to take this too seriously. It may warn us, however, not to ridicule Shakespeare for giving Bohemia a sea-coast (after Greene), or even for exchanging the names of Bohemia and Sicily in Greene's story, without any apparent reason. But we are met at the outset by a situation which, with all its beauty and pathos, severely taxes our credulity. In his handling of the jealousy of Leontes Shakespeare has deliberately rejected the rather commonplace but technically unassailable procedure of Greene. Hermione and Polixenes are both noble and honourable persons, whose cordial friendship has no thought of love, and who express their attachment only in the ways, more demonstrative than our own, then enjoined between a hostess and her guest. No differences have (so far as we learn) ever troubled her married life. Yet Leontes is made to conceive suddenly a fierce unreasoning conviction that she is false to him, a conviction which neither the moving and dignified protest of Hermione herself, nor the amazed incredulity of his court, tempers in the least degree, and which only the sentence of an oracle at last breaks down. Hermione stands alone (with Catherine) among the women of Shakespeare in the noble scorn, concealing a heart in anguish, with which she repels calumny. She does not deign, like Bellaria, to argue her innocence; nor is it she who proposes, as Bellaria does, the appeal to the oracle. This is ascribed, in the play, solely to the tardy qualms

of Leontes' conscience, hitherto completely impervious to
doubt. This may seem less likely, but Shakespeare has
made Leontes a despot of the weak and obstinate, not of
the resolutely inflexible, type; and we soon witness the
kaleidoscopic incoherence of a character which is at bottom
only a string of moods.

"I am a feather for each wind that blows", he justly
says, when struggling between the entreaties of the kneel-
ing court for his "bastard's" life, and his own savage
resolve to destroy it (ii. 3. 153):

> Shall I live on, to see this bastard kneel
> And call me father?  Better burn it now
> Than curse it then.  But be it; let it live.
> It shall not, neither.

Two other important differences tend, however, towards
greater coherence. Greene's story is an extreme example
of "wasp-like" structure—two halves attached by a very
slender thread. Shakespeare has drawn across the gap
two filaments, one of them so unobtrusive as easily to be
overlooked.

The first is the survival of Hermione. Bellaria dies;
Hermione merely swoons, and is secretly concealed in the
palace till the sixteen years have elapsed and her child has
grown up. No doubt the wonderful restoration scene at
the close was rendered possible at a cost in probability
which, outside a "Winter's Tale", would be severe. The
sixteen years' concealment in her husband's palace, unknown to him, demanded, in any case, some bold strategy
of dramatic invention if it was to be made credible at all;
and Shakespeare responded with his admirable creation
of Paulina, vigilant guardian of her royal mistress and
rough-tongued conscience to the king; a more effective
Kent or Banquo, whose sovereign quails before her fear-
less reproofs, but also the astute diplomatist who with
delicate tact prepares the way for the final solution.

The second change is slighter, but not less important.
The new-born child of Bellaria, committed to wind and

waves in an open boat, was "by chance" cast ashore on the coast of the very country where Egistus is king, and where his son will later on discover and woo her. In Shakespeare's handling of the story "Fortune" has still sufficient scope, but not quite so much as this. Antigonus is dispatched with the child, ostensibly to see that its exposure in "some remote and desert place" is duly carried out. But as they approach the coast of Bohemia, Hermione appears to him in a dream or vision and begs him to set the child ashore there. Believing that it is indeed the issue of Polixenes, and that Apollo's will, disclosed through Hermione, is that

> it should here be laid,
> Either for life or death, upon the earth
> Of its right father (iii. 3. 44 *f.*),

Antigonus complies. It is thus, in so far, no accident that Perdita is then discovered by the "Bohemian" shepherd who brings her up. Some other slighter changes designed to temper the fortuitousness of this too "romantic" episode, are specified in the notes.

§ 6. The great pastoral scene of the fourth act is the most wonderful example in the play of Shakespeare's transforming power. The transformation is not all of one kind. Greene's pastoral world is a literary product, distilled with no great skill from the tradition of literary pastoral; simulating the actual world, but with hardly a touch of observation and no touch of poetry. Shakespeare gives us both observation and poetry, actuality and imagination; now detached and contrasted, as in the homely and empty-headed Mopsa and Dorcas beside Perdita; now charmingly blended, as in Autolycus. The old shepherd's description of his dead wife playing hostess at rural festivals in bygone days is a delicious vignette—a Flemish scene by Frans Hals in an English setting. Her robust geniality sets off with exquisite effect Perdita's shy and reticent grace. Autolycus belongs to both worlds. He is a light-hearted and light-fingered rogue of the English country-side, to whom the simple farmers' daughters and their clownish swains fall an easy prey. Like Touchstone, too, he has served at court, "though now out of service", and can put on the courtier's airs and phrases to perfection when a simpleton is to be bamboozled. But this merry rascal was really "littered under Mercury", and we may believe that that planet flashed and twinkled at the sight, as "a star danced" at the birth of Beatrice. A poet shares his joyous heart with the pilferer, and their rival strains come from his lips delightfully mingled in the jocund rhymes of his spring song—that incomparable welcome to the season "sweet of the year", when white sheets lie bleaching on the hedge, and daffodils begin to peer in the meadow, and the lark sings tirra-lirra overhead.

But with the appearance of Florizel and Perdita another strain begins; their opening colloquy, nobly choice yet simple in diction and thought, as in verse music, reaches the highest level of pastoral idyll. There is no more than the bare situation in Greene. But the sequel, where Polixenes and Camillo appear as unknown onlookers, gives rise both to a yet richer and deeper poetry and to an acute dramatic tension, of which Greene has no hint. Most of the poetry is directly or indirectly inspired by Perdita, some of it flows spontaneously from her own untaught lips; and the dramatic tension interests us chiefly because of the beautiful simplicity with which she meets it, let us rather say that for her there is no tension at all, so instantly, on the discovery of Florizel's rank, does she surrender her maiden dream of love. If she leaves a slighter impression upon the imagination than Imogen, her nearest of kin among Shakespeare's women, it is only because her budding womanhood is less sorely tried and has less opportunity for tragic suffering or heroic response; she is not less exquisitely imagined. And while Imogen, even in her disguise, is aware of her origin, Perdita's inborn fineness of breed distils itself spontaneously through the homely trappings of her shepherdess's status. She is deeply in love with Florizel, but her passion, too delicate

and reticent for direct expression, finds utterance only
through the silent symbolism of flowers—primroses that
die unmarried, violets sweeter than Cytherea's breath, and
those that Proserpina let fall in fright at the clasp of her
awful lover from the shades below.   She would fain
guerdon the whole company with flowers, but it is for
Florizel that she secretly means them, and at the close
her shy disguise falls away:

> O these I lack,
> To make you garlands of, and my sweet friend,
> To strew him o'er and o'er.

"What, like a corse?" he asks, and then the image of a
flower-crowned bridal with him suddenly possesses her,
and she yields to it with an ecstasy which breaks through
all reserves:

> No, like a bank for love to lie and play on;
> Not like a corse; or if, not to be buried,
> But quick and in mine arms.

But she immediately stops short, and hastily resumes her
flower-gifts, pleading that she was like a Whitsun player,
acting a part:

> Sure this robe of mine
> Does change my disposition.

In her famous colloquy with Polixenes, just before, idyll
reaches a note of grave philosophic reflexion quite beyond
the scope or the resources of Pastoral literature; while the
presence of Polixenes with Camillo as apparently bene-
volent witnesses of the innocent merry-making, which
they are presently to wreck, creates a background of irony
for the lovers' talk, somewhat like that of which we are
conscious when the king and Polonius listen behind the
arras to Hamlet and Ophelia's suspected "love".   But the
irony, as Prof. Moorman (Arden ed., p. 75), has pointed
out, is not confined to the lovers, unsuspicious as they
are of their impending fate.   Polixenes himself, the philo-
sopher who so loftily refutes (without disturbing) the shep-

herd maid's simple faith, presently justifies her by his own
action. The pied gillyvor, he urges, grown by grafting
"a bud of nobler race" upon "a bark of baser kind", is
not to be condemned as unnatural; for the art which
changes nature is itself nature. But "before the scene is
over, we witness the ungovernable fury of Polixenes that
the 'gentler scion' that has sprung from his own loins
should marry the 'wild stock' that has grown up in the
home of the shepherd".

The escape of the lovers to Sicily is lightly treated. The
misfortunes of lovers by land and sea, a stock incident of
romance, were of little interest to the mature Shakespeare,
and he uses the escape chiefly as further occasion for the
versatile knaveries of Autolycus (his own creation) at the
cost of the simple shepherds.

§ 7. Shakespeare's fifth act opens in Sicily, and everything in it is subordinated to the great recognition scene
at the close. The opening words foreshadow the end of
the king's long penance. "Sir, you have done enough",
he is told, "and have performed a saint-like sorrow."
The court begin to betray concern at the absence of an
heir, and openly urge a second marriage. Paulina, driven
to bay, extorts from the now submissive king a promise
to take only a wife whom she will provide. Everything is
prepared for the great *dénouement*—the reunion of wife
and husband.

The arrival of Florizel and Perdita, soon followed by that
of Polixenes, introduces a new and exciting complication,
which threatens to bring the drama to a less harmonious
consummation. And it would not have been un-Shakespearean to keep the reader in suspense, even in a fifth act,
with incidents which retard, or run actually counter to,
the evident drift of the action. So in the last scene of
*Cymbeline*, when Iachimo is forgiven and Imogen restored
to her husband, tragedy suddenly menaces again: Arviragus is sent to death, and Belarius is about to follow him,
when a final recognition saves them all. Four or five distinct stories engage us almost equally in this single scene.

In the fifth act of our play (so rash it is to generalize about Shakespeare's technique even in the same group of plays), the dramatist adopts a quite different procedure. He seems here resolved to keep all the rival interests, which his own rich and brilliant fourth act has generated, from competing seriously with the great climax which is to solve the tragic imbroglio unfolded in the first three. Greene had no such climax; Dorastus and Fawnia were now sole hero and heroine, and he exposes them, as we saw, with her shepherd father, to further sensational perils before the final disclosure. Shakespeare, in the first place, dismisses wholly the tasteless episode of the king's violent love-making to his unknown daughter, as well as his sub-sequent savage condemnation of her when he discovers her mean birth. Leontes is from the outset won by the charm and beauty of the young people, and when he hears of Perdita's lowly origin, offers himself as their friend to plead their cause with Florizel's irate father. Then follows the old shepherd's disclosure; but this dramatic climax, instead of being made in our presence, like its counter-parts in *Cymbeline*, is merely reported to us by the talk of "gentlemen", and this in an affected court dialect, wholly denuded of poetry or beauty. The close of the scene plea-santly and briefly disposes of the shepherd, now rewarded for his fidelity. Then follows the real consummation, which the coming and discovery of Perdita has not so much retarded as enriched. For the mother is to be re-stored to the daughter whom she has not seen since infancy, as well as the wife to the husband; and this recovery, not less beautiful and moving in itself, is also far rarer, if not quite unexampled, in Shakespeare. Almost all his heroines, for excellent dramatic reasons, are without a living mother.[1] Even more startling, however, is Shakespeare's resort, for his recognition scene, to the device of the supposed statue,

---

[1] The first editions of *Much Ado about Nothing* have a stage direction, "Enter Leonato, . . . Innogen his wife"; but there is no other trace of Hero's mother in the play. This may have been Shakespeare's first thought, accidentally left uncancelled.

presented as Hermione's life-like portrait. The solution superficially resembles that in *Much Ado*, where Hero, "done to death by slanderous tongues", is restored to Claudio in the person, as he supposes, of her cousin. But the handling of that reunion is singularly dry and perfunctory, and we forget it a moment later in the last gay encounter of Benedict and Beatrice. In the early and middle comedies the reunion of kin, or of husband and wife, where it occurs at all, has rarely any emotional significance. Not to mention the farcical close of *Two Gentlemen*, we may recall Rosalind's reunion with her father — just one item in the merry unmasking which crowns her brilliant jest. It is only in the latest group of comedies that these meetings of separated kin or estranged companions are drawn with pathos; and here the pathos is sometimes, as in the meeting of Postumus and Imogen, and in the present scene, of an overpowering intensity with which we can only compare Othello's ineffable welcome to Desdemona (ii. 1), after only two days' separation and with nothing to forgive on either side. The meeting of Postumus and Imogen, and the reunion here, have in common that they are reached after a period of illusion. But in *Cymbeline* the illusion is a cruel misunderstanding (Postumus strikes down the "scornful page" in the very moment of uttering his anguished remorse for his "villany" to her); whereas here the illusion, merely the enthralling illusion of a seemingly life-like work of art, is slowly, by delicate and gradual steps, dissolved. Even the great moment, one of the most thrilling single moments in Shakespeare, when Paulina calls to the waiting musicians:

> Music, awake her, strike!
> 'T is time; descend; be stone no more; approach,

does not completely dissolve it. Even when Hermione has slowly stepped down, and is offering to embrace Leontes, he stands petrified with wonder; and even when he feels her arms about his neck, he doubts whether some magic has not made the statue warm. She does not speak, and no one but Paulina addresses her. It is only when Perdita kneels at her feet that her tongue is unloosed. Leontes only in the final speech of the play finds words to address her in a final plea for pardon.

§ 8. *The Winter's Tale* thus closes, not with those incredible changes of fortune which had so largely occupied it, but with a scene of purely natural "magic", where husband and wife, mother and daughter, are restored to one another by the "worth and honesty", the wit and patience, of one devoted woman. Paulina, Shakespeare's creation, has triumphantly carried her difficult project through. But its success is far more than a personal triumph. She plays the part in this drama, as Prospero does in *The Tempest* and Belarius and his boys in *Cymbeline*, of an earthly providence, intervening in the action at its most critical point to forestall disaster and turn the menacing perils to a happy issue. All these figures are drawn with an idealistic touch rare outside this latest group of plays. None of them approaches the abstractions of allegory; but their warm and rich humanity seems to have no stain of evil; they all unconsciously embody, to our eyes, the benign forces of the world. These benign forces are associated, it is true, with different aspects or regions of it. In Guiderius and Arviragus it is the nobility of unspoilt youth; in Prospero the nobility of wise and humane maturity. In Paulina it is the nobility of large-hearted, sagacious, and energetic womanhood.

We must beware of discovering conscious moral intention or tendency in Shakespeare's plays. But it is hard to resist the impression that the poet who in *The Winter's Tale* drew goodness in women—heroic in suffering, powerful to help, or intuitively wise—with a sympathetic insight so tender and so pronounced as he shows in Hermione, Paulina, and Perdita, is separated by something deeper than a change of theatrical fashion from the poet who in *Macbeth*, *Antony and Cleopatra*, and *Troilus and Cressida* had pictured with a peculiar intensity the malign power of a woman over a man, and shown even women of ideal goodness and purity, by an innocent but fatal blindness contributing to bring about their own tragic doom. Desdemona runs blindly into Iago's net; Hermione, as clear-eyed as she is innocent, is blindly thrust by Leontes into his own. But here, as goodness is more potent and more prevailing, so the harms are less deadly and more medicable; and the scene closes in a harmony yet richer and less touched with dissonance than we experience in the companion dramas, where the solemn joy of reunion is disturbed by the death-dealing rage of Cymbeline, only just allayed, or by the menace of a base conspiracy, only just discovered.

# THE WINTER'S TALE

# DRAMATIS PERSONÆ

LEONTES, king of Sicilia.

MAMILLIUS, young prince of Sicilia.

CAMILLO,
ANTIGONUS,
CLEOMENES,
DION,
} four Lords of Sicilia.

POLIXENES, king of Bohemia.

FLORIZEL, prince of Bohemia.

ARCHIDAMUS, a Lord of Bohemia.

Old Shepherd, reputed father of Perdita.

Clown, his son.

AUTOLYCUS, a rogue.

A Mariner.

A Gaoler.

HERMIONE, queen to Leontes.

PERDITA, daughter to Leontes and Hermione.

PAULINA, wife to Antigonus.

EMILIA, a lady attending on Hermione.

MOPSA,
DORCAS,
} Shepherdesses.

Other Lords and Gentlemen, Ladies, Officers, and Servants
Shepherds and Shepherdesses.

Time, as Chorus

Scene: *Sicilia and Bohemia*

# THE WINTER'S TALE

## ACT I

### Scene I. *Antechamber in Leontes' palace*

*Enter* Camillo *and* Archidamus

*Arch.* If you shall chance, Camillo, to visit Bohemia, on the like occasion whereon my services are now on foot, you shall see, as I have said, great difference betwixt our Bohemia and your Sicilia.

*Cam.* I think, this coming summer, the King of Sicilia means to pay Bohemia the visitation which he justly owes him.

*Arch.* Wherein our entertainment shall shame us we will be justified in our loves; for indeed—

*Cam.* Beseech you,—                                                10

*Arch.* Verily, I speak it in the freedom of my knowledge: we cannot with such magnificence—in so rare—I know not what to say. We will give you sleepy drinks, that your senses, unintelligent of our insufficience, may, though they cannot praise us, as little accuse us.

*Cam.* You pay a great deal too dear for what's given freely.

*Arch.* Believe me, I speak as my understanding instructs me, and as mine honesty puts it to utterance. 20

1

*Kings* [handwritten]

*Cam.* Sicilia cannot show himself over-kind to Bohemia.    They were train'd together in their childhood;
and there rooted betwixt them then such an affection,
which cannot choose but branch now.    Since their more
mature dignities and royal necessities made separation
of their society, their encounters, though not personal,
have been royally attorneyed with interchange of gifts,
letters, loving embassies; that they have seem'd to be
together, though absent; shook hands, as over a vast;
and embrac'd, as it were, from the ends of opposed
winds.    The heavens continue their loves!    31

*Arch.* I think there is not in the world either malice
or matter to alter it.    You have an unspeakable comfort
of your young prince Mamillius: it is a gentleman of
the greatest promise that ever came into my note.

*Cam.* I very well agree with you in the hopes of him:
it is a gallant child; one that, indeed, physics the subject, makes old hearts fresh: they that went on crutches
ere he was born desire yet their life to see him a man.

*Arch.* Would they else be content to die?    40

*Cam.* Yes; if there were no other excuse why they
should desire to live.

*Arch.* If the king had no son, they would desire to
live on crutches till he had one.    [*Exeunt.*

SCENE II.    *A state-room in Leontes' palace*

*Enter* LEONTES, HERMIONE, MAMILLIUS,
POLIXENES, CAMILLO, *and* Attendants

*Room* [handwritten]

*Pol.* Nine changes of the watery star hath been
The shepherd's note since we have left our throne    *No one*
Without a burden: time as long again    *setting*
Would be fill'd up, my brother, with our thanks;    *on it*
And yet we should, for perpetuity,
Go hence in debt: and therefore, like a cipher,

*not long enough to let us express our gratitude* [handwritten]

Yet standing in rich place, I multiply
With one " We-thank-you " many thousands moe
That go before it.                *10 times over*
   *Leon.*        Stay your thanks awhile,
And pay them when you part.
   *Pol.*             Sir, that 's to-morrow. 10
I am question'd by my fears, of what may chance
Or breed upon our absence; that may blow
No sneaping winds at home, to make us say,
" This is put forth too truly:" besides, I have stay'd
To tire your royalty.
   *Leon.*      We are tougher, brother,
Than you can put us to 't.
   *Pol.*          No longer stay.
   *Leon.* One seven-night longer.
   *Pol.*          Very sooth, to-morrow.
   *Leon.* We 'll part the time between 's, then: and in that
I 'll no gainsaying.
   *Pol.*        Press me not, beseech you, so.
There is no tongue that moves, none, none i' the world,
So soon as yours, could win me: so it should now,   21
Were there necessity in your request, although
'T were needful I denied it.   My affairs
Do even drag me homeward: which to hinder,
Were in your love a whip to me; my stay,
To you a charge and trouble: to save both,
Farewell, our brother.
   *Leon.*        Tongue-tied our queen? speak you.
   *Her.* I had thought, sir, to have held my peace until
You had drawn oaths from him not to stay.   You, sir,
Charge him too coldly.   Tell him, you are sure   30
All in Bohemia 's well; this satisfaction
The by-gone day proclaim'd: say this to him,
He 's beat from his best ward.
   *Leon.*          Well said, Hermione.

*Her.* To tell, he longs to see his son, were strong:
But let him say so then, and let him go;
But let him swear so, and he shall not stay,
We 'll thwack him hence with distaffs.
Yet of your royal presence I 'll adventure
The borrow of a week.   When at Bohemia
You take my lord, I 'll give him my commission          40
To let him there a month behind the gest
Prefix'd for 's parting: yet, good deed, Leontes,
I love thee not a jar o' the clock behind
What lady she her lord.   You 'll stay?
  *Pol.*        No, madam.
  *Her.* Nay, but you will?
  *Pol.*      I may not, verily.
  *Her.* Verily!
You put me off with limber vows; but I,
Though you would seek to unsphere the stars with oaths,
Should yet say, " Sir, no going."   Verily,
You shall not go: a lady's " verily " is          50
As potent as a lord's.   Will you go yet?
Force me to keep you as a prisoner,
Not like a guest: so you shall pay your fees
When you depart, and save your thanks.   How say you?
My prisoner, or my guest? by your dread " verily ",
One of them you shall be.
  *Pol.*     Your guest, then, madam:
To be your prisoner should import offending;
Which is for me less easy to commit
Than you to punish.
  *Her.*    Not your gaoler, then,
But your kind hostess.   Come, I 'll question you          60
Of my lord's tricks and yours when you were boys:
You were pretty lordings then?
  *Pol.*     We were, fair queen,
Two lads that thought there was no more behind

But such a day to-morrow as to-day,
And to be boy eternal.
    *Her.*                     Was not my lord
The verier wag o' the two?
    *Pol.* We were as twinn'd lambs that did frisk i' the
        sun,
And bleat the one at the other: what we chang'd
Was innocence for innocence; we knew not
The doctrine of ill-doing, no, nor dream'd           70
That any did.   Had we pursued that life,
And our weak spirits ne'er been higher rear'd
With stronger blood, we should have answer'd heaven
Boldly, "not guilty;" the imposition clear'd
Hereditary ours.
    *Her.*              By this we gather
You have tripp'd since.
    *Pol.*                     O my most sacred lady,
Temptations have since then been born to 's; for
In those unfledg'd days was my wife a girl;
Your precious self had then not cross'd the eyes
Of my young playfellow.
    *Her.*                       Grace to boot!           80
Of this make no conclusion, lest you say
Your queen and I are devils: yet go on;
The offences we have made you do, we 'll answer,
If you first sinn'd with us, and that with us
You did continue fault, and that you slipp'd not
With any but with us.
    *Leon.*              Is he won yet?
    *Her.* He 'll stay, my lord.
    *Leon.*                     At my request he would not.
Hermione, my dearest, thou never spok'st
To better purpose.
    *Her.*        Never?
    *Leon.*                Never, but once.

*Her.* What! have I twice said well; when was 't
    before?                                                                    90
I prithee tell me; cram 's with praise, and make 's
As fat as tame things: one good deed dying tongueless
Slaughters a thousand waiting upon that.
Our praises are our wages: you may ride 's
With one soft kiss a thousand furlongs ere
With spur we heat an acre.   But to the goal:
My last good deed was to entreat his stay:
What was my first?   it has an elder sister,
Or I mistake you: O would her name were Grace!
But once before I spoke to the purpose: when?        100
Nay, let me have 't; I long.
   *Leon.*                         Why, that was when
Three crabbed months had sour'd themselves to death,
Ere I could make thee open thy white hand,
And clap thyself my love: then didst thou utter,
" I am yours for ever."
   *Her.*                        'T is Grace indeed.
Why, lo you now, I have spoke to the purpose twice:
The one for ever earn'd a royal husband;
The other for some while a friend.
   *Leon.*  [*Aside*]                 Too hot, too hot!
To mingle friendship far, is mingling bloods.
I have *tremor cordis* on me; my heart dances;        110
But not for joy; not joy.   This entertainment
May a free face put on; derive a liberty
From heartiness, from bounty, fertile bosom,
And well become the agent; 't may, I grant;
But to be paddling palms and pinching fingers,
As now they are, and making practis'd smiles,
As in a looking-glass; and then to sigh, as 't were
The mort o' the deer; O, that is entertainment
My bosom likes not, nor my brows!   Mamillius,
Art thou my boy?
                                  (D 656)

*Mam.*          Ay, my good lord.

*Leon.*          I' fecks!          120
Why, that's my bawcock.  What, has smutch'd thy
   nose?
They say it is a copy out of mine.  Come, captain:
We must be neat; not neat, but cleanly, captain:
And yet the steer, the heifer, and the calf,
Are all call'd neat.—Still virginalling
Upon his palm!—How now, you wanton calf?
Art thou my calf?

*Mam.*          Yes, if you will, my lord.

*Leon.*  Thou want'st a rough pash, and the shoots that
   I have,
To be full like me: yet they say we are
Almost as like as eggs; women say so,          130
That will say any thing: but were they false
As o'er-dyed blacks, as wind, as waters, false
As dice are to be wish'd by one that fixes
No bourn 'twixt his and mine, yet were it true
To say this boy were like me.  Come, sir page,
Look on me with your welkin eye: sweet villain!
Most dear'st! my collop!  Can thy dam?—may 't be?—
Affection! thy intention stabs the centre:
Thou dost make possible things not so held,
Communicat'st with dreams;—how can this be?—          140
With what 's unreal thou coactive art,
And fellow'st nothing: then 't is very credent
Thou mayst co-join with something; and thou dost,
And that beyond commission, and I find it,
And that to the infection of my brains
And hardening of my brows.

*Pol.*                    What means Sicilia?

*Her.*  He something seems unsettled.

*Pol.*                              How, my lord!

*Leon.*  What cheer? how is 't with you, best brother?

2          (D 656)

*Her.*                                              You look
As if you held a brow of much distraction:
Are you mov'd, my lord?

    *Leon.*                    No, in good earnest.        150
How sometimes nature will betray its folly,
Its tenderness, and make itself a pastime
To harder bosoms!   Looking on the lines
Of my boy's face, methoughts I did recoil
Twenty-three years, and saw myself unbreech'd,
In my green velvet coat, my dagger muzzled,
Lest it should bite its master, and so prove,
As ornaments oft do, too dangerous:
How like, methought, I then was to this kernel,
This squash, this gentleman.   Mine honest friend,   160
Will you take eggs for money?

    *Mam.* No, my lord, I 'll fight.

    *Leon.* You will? why, happy man be 's dole!   My
      brother,
Are you so fond of your young prince as we
Do seem to be of ours?

    *Pol.*                    If at home, sir,
He 's all my exercise, my mirth, my matter;
Now my sworn friend, and then mine enemy;
My parasite, my soldier, statesman, all:
He makes a July's day short as December;
And with his varying childness cures in me        170
Thoughts that would thick my blood.

    *Leon.*                        So stands this squire
Officed with me.   We two will walk, my lord,
And leave you to your graver steps.   Hermione,
How thou lov'st us, show in our brother's welcome;
Let what is dear in Sicily be cheap:
Next to thyself and my young rover, he 's
Apparent to my heart.

    *Her.*                    If you would seek us,

We are yours i' the garden: shall 's attend you there?

*Leon.* To your own bents dispose you: you'll be found.
Be you beneath the sky. [*Aside*] I am angling now,    180
Though you perceive me not how I give line.
Go to, go to!
How she holds up the neb, the bill to him!
And arms her with the boldness of a wife
To her allowing husband!

[*Exeunt Polixenes, Hermione, and Attendants.*
                                    Gone already!
Inch-thick, knee-deep, o'er head and ears a fork'd one!
Go, play, boy, play: thy mother plays, and I
Play too; but so disgraced a part, whose issue
Will hiss me to my grave: contempt and clamour
Will be my knell.   Go, play, boy, play.    190
Should all despair
That have revolted wives, the tenth of mankind
Would hang themselves.   Physic for 't there is none;
How now, boy!

*Mam.* I am like you, they say.
*Leon.*                    Why, that's some comfort.
What, Camillo there?

*Cam.*                Ay, my good lord.
*Leon.* Go, play, Mamillius; thou 'rt an honest man.

[*Exit Mamillius.*
Camillo, this great sir will yet stay longer.

*Cam.* You had much ado to make his anchor hold:
When you cast out, it still came home.

*Leon.*                            Didst note it?
*Cam.* He would not stay at your petitions; made    201
His business more material.

*Leon.*                    Didst perceive it?—
[*Aside*] They're here with me already; whispering,
    rounding,
"Sicilia is a—so-forth:" 't is far gone,

When I shall gust it last.   How came 't, Camillo,
That he did stay?
    *Cam.*             At the good queen's entreaty.
    *Leon.* At the queen's be 't: "good" should be per-
    tinent;
But, so it is, it is not.   Was this taken
By any understanding pate but thine?
For thy conceit is soaking, will draw in        210
More than the common blocks: not noted, is 't,
But of the finer natures? by some severals
Of head-piece extraordinary? lower messes
Perchance are to this business purblind? say.
    *Cam.*   Business, my lord?   I think most understand
Bohemia stays here longer.
    *Leon.*             Ha!
    *Cam.*                  Stays here longer.
    *Leon.* Ay, but why?
    *Cam.* To satisfy your highness, and the entreaties
Of our most gracious mistress.
    *Leon.*              Satisfy
The entreaties of your mistress? satisfy?      220
Let that suffice.   I have trusted thee, Camillo,
With all the nearest things to my heart, as well
My chamber-councils; wherein, priest-like, thou
Hast cleans'd my bosom, I from thee departed
Thy penitent reform'd: but we have been
Deceiv'd in thy integrity, deceiv'd
In that which seems so.
    *Cam.*          Be it forbid, my lord!
    *Leon.* To bide upon 't, thou art not honest; or,
If thou inclin'st that way, thou art a coward,
Which hoxes honesty behind, restraining      230
From course requir'd; or else thou must be counted
A servant grafted in my serious trust,
And therein negligent; or else a fool

That seest a game play'd home, the rich stake drawn,
And tak'st it all for jest.
    *Cam.*              My gracious lord,
I may be negligent, foolish, and fearful;
In every one of these no man is free,
But that his negligence, his folly, fear,
Among the infinite doings of the world,
Sometime puts forth.   In your affairs, my lord,    240
If ever I were wilful-negligent,
It was my folly; if industriously
I play'd the fool, it was my negligence,
Not weighing well the end; if ever fearful
To do a thing, where I the issue doubted,
Whereof the execution did cry out
Against the non-performance, 't was a fear
Which oft infects the wisest: these, my lord,
Are such allow'd infirmities that honesty
Is never free of.   But, beseech your grace,    250
Be plainer with me; let me know my trespass
By its own visage: if I then deny it,
'T is none of mine.
    *Leon.*         Ha' not you seen, Camillo,—
Or heard,—
For, to a vision so apparent, rumour
Cannot be mute,—or thought,—for cogitation
Resides not in that man that does not think,—
My wife is slippery? If thou wilt confess,
Or else be impudently negative,
To have nor eyes nor ears nor thought, then    260
Say 't and justify 't.
    *Cam.*  I would not be a stander-by to hear
My sovereign mistress clouded so, without
My present vengeance taken: 'shrew my heart,
You never spoke what did become you less
Than this, which to reiterate were sin

As deep as that, though true.

    *Leon.*                       Is whispering nothing?
Is leaning cheek to cheek? is meeting noses?
Kissing with inside lip? stopping the career
Of laughter with a sigh?—a note infallible     270
Of breaking honesty;—horsing foot on foot?
Skulking in corners? wishing clocks more swift?
Hours, minutes? noon, midnight? and all eyes
Blind with the pin and web, but theirs, theirs only,
That would unseen be wicked? is this nothing?
Why, then the world and all that's in't is nothing;
The covering sky is nothing; Bohemia nothing;
My wife is nothing; nor nothing have these nothings,
If this be nothing.

    *Cam.*           Good my lord, be cured
Of this diseas'd opinion, and betimes;     280
For 't is most dangerous.

    *Leon.*            Say it be, 't is true.

    *Cam.* No, no, my lord.

    *Leon.*             It is; you lie, you lie:
I say thou liest, Camillo, and I hate thee,
Pronounce thee a gross lout, a mindless slave,
Or else a hovering temporizer, that
Canst with thine eyes at once see good and evil,
Inclining to them both: were my wife's liver
Infected as her life, she would not live
The running of one glass.

    *Cam.*           Who does infect her?

    *Leon.* Why, he that wears her like her medal, hanging
About his neck, Bohemia: who, if I     291
Had servants true about me, that bare eyes
To see alike mine honour as their profits,
Their own particular thrifts, they would do that
Which should undo more doing: ay, and thou,
His cupbearer,—whom I from meaner form

Have bench'd and rear'd to worship, who mayst see
Plainly, as heaven sees earth and earth sees heaven,
How I am gall'd,—mightst bespice a cup,
To give mine enemy a lasting wink;                    300
Which draught to me were cordial.
   *Cam.*                  Sir, my lord,
I could do this, and that with no rash potion,
But with a lingering dram, that should not work
Maliciously like poison: but I cannot
Believe this crack to be in my dread mistress,
So sovereignly being honourable.
I have lov'd thee,—
   *Leon.* Make that thy question, and go rot!
Dost think I am so muddy, so unsettled,
To appoint myself in this vexation; sully            310
The purity and whiteness of my sheets,
Which to preserve is sleep, which being spotted
Is goads, thorns, nettles, tails of wasps;
Give scandal to the blood o' the prince my son,
Who I do think is mine, and love as mine,
Without ripe moving to 't?   Would I do this?
Could man so blench?
   *Cam.*           I must believe you, sir:
I do; and will fetch off Bohemia for 't;
Provided that, when he 's remov'd, your highness
Will take again your queen as yours at first,        320
Even for your son's sake; and thereby for sealing
The injury of tongues in courts and kingdoms
Known and allied to yours.
   *Leon.*           Thou dost advise me
Even so as I mine own course have set down:
I 'll give no blemish to her honour, none.
   *Cam.* My, lord,
Go then; and with a countenance as clear
As friendship wears at feasts, keep with Bohemia

And with your queen.   I am his cupbearer:
If from me he have wholesome beverage,                    330
Account me not your servant.

   *Leon.*                              This is all:
Do 't, and thou hast the one half of my heart;
Do 't not, thou splitt'st thine own.

    *Cam.*                              I 'll do 't, my lord.

    *Leon.* I will seem friendly, as thou hast advis'd me.

                         [*Exit.*

    *Cam.* O miserable lady!   But, for me,
What case stand I in?   I must be the poisoner
Of good Polixenes: and my ground to do 't
Is the obedience to a master; one
Who, in rebellion with himself, will have
All that are his so too.   To do this deed,                  340
Promotion follows: if I could find example
Of thousands that had struck anointed kings
And flourish'd after, I 'd not do 't; but since
Nor brass nor stone nor parchment bears not one,
Let villany itself forswear 't.   I must
Forsake the court: to do 't, or no, is certain
To me a break-neck.   Happy star reign now!
Here comes Bohemia.

           *Re-enter* POLIXENES

   *Pol.*                              This is strange: methinks
My favour here begins to warp.   Not speaks?
Good day, Camillo.

    *Cam.*                    Hail, most royal sir!                    350

    *Pol.* What is the news i' the court?

    *Cam.*                              None rare, my lord.

    *Pol.* The king hath on him such a countenance
As he had lost some province, and a region
Lov'd as he loves himself: even now I met him

With customary compliment; when he,
Wafting his eyes to the contrary, and falling
A lip of much contempt, speeds from me, and
So leaves me, to consider what is breeding
That changes thus his manners.

   *Cam.* I dare not know, my lord,                    360
   *Pol.* How! dare not? do not? Do you know, and
     dare not?
Be intelligent to me. 'T is thereabouts;
For, to yourself, what you do know, you must,
And cannot say you dare not. Good Camillo,
Your chang'd complexions are to me a mirror,
Which shows me mine chang'd too; for I must be
A party in this alteration, finding
Myself thus alter'd with 't.

   *Cam.*                    There is a sickness
Which puts some of us in distemper; but
I cannot name the disease; and it is caught                    370
Of you that yet are well.

   *Pol.*                    How! caught of me?
Make me not sighted like the basilisk:
I have look'd on thousands, who have sped the better
By my regard, but kill'd none so. Camillo,—
As you are certainly a gentleman; thereto
Clerk-like experienced, which no less adorns
Our gentry than our parents' noble names,
In whose success we are gentle,—I beseech you,
If you know aught which does behove my knowledge
Thereof to be inform'd, imprison 't not                    380
In ignorant concealment.

   *Cam.*                    I may not answer,
   *Pol.* A sickness caught of me, and yet I well.
I must be answer'd. Dost thou hear, Camillo,
I cónjure thee, by all the parts of man
Which honour does acknowledge, whereof the least

2*

Is not this suit of mine, that thou declare
What incidency thou dost guess of harm
Is creeping toward me; how far off, how near;
Which way to be prevented, if to be;
If not, how best to bear it.

 *Cam.*       Sir, I will tell you; 390
Since I am charged in honour, and by him
That I think honourable: therefore mark my counsel,
Which must be even as swiftly follow'd as
I mean to utter 't, or both yourself and me
Cry " lost ", and so good night!

 *Pol.*       On, good Camillo.

 *Cam.* I am appointed him to murder you.

 *Pol.* By whom, Camillo?

 *Cam.*    By the king.

 *Pol.*        For what?

 *Cam.* He thinks, nay, with all confidence he swears,
As he had seen 't, or been an instrument
To vice you to 't, that you have touch'd his queen 400
Forbiddenly.

 *Pol.*   O, then my best blood turn
To an infected jelly, and my name
Be yoked with his that did betray the Best!
Turn then my freshest reputation to
A savour that may strike the dullest nostril
Where I arrive, and my approach be shunn'd,
Nay, hated too, worse than the great'st infection
That e'er was heard or read!

 *Cam.*    Swear his thoughts over
By each particular star in heaven and
By all their influences, you may as well 410
Forbid the sea for to obey the moon,
As or by oath remove or counsel shake
The fabric of his folly, whose foundation
Is piled upon his faith, and will continue

The standing of his body.
   *Pol.*               How should this grow?
   *Cam.* I know not: but I 'm sure 't is safer to
Avoid what 's grown than question how 't is born.
If, therefore, you dare trust my honesty,
That lies enclosed in this trunk which you
Shall bear along impawn'd, away to-night!       420
Your followers I will whisper to the business;
And will by twos and threes at several posterns
Clear them o' the city: for myself, I 'll put
My fortunes to your service, which are here
By this discovery lost.   Be not uncertain;
For, by the honour of my parents, I
Have utter'd truth: which if you seek to prove,
I dare not stand by; nor shall you be safer
Than one condemn'd by the king's own mouth, thereon
His execution sworn.
   *Pol.*          I do believe thee:   430
I saw his heart in 's face.   Give me thy hand:
Be pilot to me, and thy places shall
Still neighbour mine.   My ships are ready and
My people did expect my hence departure
Two days ago.   This jealousy
Is for a precious creature: as she 's rare,
Must it be great; and, as his person 's mighty,
Must it be violent; and as he does conceive
He is dishonour'd by a man which ever
Profess'd to him, why, his revenges must     440
In that be made more bitter.   Fear o'ershades me:
Good expedition be my friend, and comfort
The gracious queen, part of his theme, but nothing
Of his ill-ta'en suspicion!   Come, Camillo;
I will respect thee as a father if
Thou bear'st my life off hence: let us avoid.
   *Cam.* It is in mine authority to command

The keys of all the posterns; please your highness
To take the urgent hour. Come, sir, away.          [*Exeunt.*

---

## ACT II

### Scene I.    *A room in Leontes' palace*

#### *Enter* Hermione, Mamillius, *and* Ladies

*Her.* Take the boy to you: he so troubles me,
'T is past enduring.
    *First Lady.*          Come, my gracious lord,
Shall I be your playfellow?
    *Mam.*                    No, I 'll none of you.
    *First Lady.* Why, my sweet lord?
    *Mam.* You 'll kiss me hard, and speak to me **as if**
I were a baby still. I love you better.
    *Sec. Lady.* And why so, my lord?
    *Mam.*                    Not for because
Your brows are blacker; yet black brows, they say,
Become some women best, so that there be not
Too much hair there, but in a semicircle,          10
Or a half-moon made with a pen.
    *Sec. Lady.*                    Who taught you this?
    *Mam.* I learn'd it out of women's faces. Pray now
What colour are your eyebrows?
    *First Lady.*                    Blue, my lord.
    *Mam.* Nay, that 's a mock: I 've seen a lady's nose
That has been blue, but not her eyebrows.
    *First Lady.*                    Hark ye;
The queen your mother rounds apace: we shall
Present our services to a fine new prince
One of these days; and then you 'd wanton with us,
If we would have you.

*Sec. Lady.* She is spread of late
Into a goodly bulk: good time encounter her! 20
 *Her.* What wisdom stirs amongst you? Come, sir,
  now
I am for you again: pray you, sit by us,
And tell's a tale.
 *Mam.* Merry or sad shall't be?
 *Her.* As merry as you will.
 *Mam.* A sad tale's best for winter: I have one
Of sprites and goblins.
 *Her.* Let's have that, good sir.
Come, on, sit down: come on, and do your best
To fright me with your sprites; you're powerful at it.
 *Mam.* There was a man—
 *Her.* Nay, come, sit down; then on.
 *Mam.* Dwelt by a churchyard: I will tell it softly; 30
Yond crickets shall not hear it.
 *Her.* Come on, then,
And give't me in mine ear.

  *Enter* LEONTES, ANTIGONUS, Lords, *and* Guards

 *Leon.* Was he met there? his train? Camillo with him?
 *First Lord.* Behind the tuft of pines I met them; never
Saw I men scour so on their way: I eyed them
Even to their ships.
 *Leon.* How blest am I
In my just censure, in my true opinion!
Alack for lesser knowledge! how accurs'd
In being so blest! There may be in the cup
A spider steep'd, and one may drink, depart, 40
And yet partake no venom; for his knowledge
Is not infected: but if one present
The abhorred ingredient to his eye, make known
How he hath drunk, he cracks his gorge, his sides,
With violent hefts. I have drunk, and seen the spider.

Camillo was his help in this, his pander:
There is a plot against my life, my crown;
All's true that is mistrusted: that false villain
Whom I employ'd was pre-employ'd by him:
He has discover'd my design, and I          *disclosed*          50
Remain a pinch'd thing; yea, a very trick   *tricked*
For them to play at will.   How came the posterns
So easily open?

   *First Lord.*    By his great authority;
Which often hath no less prevail'd than so
On your command.

   *Leon.*          I know 't too well.
Give me the boy: I am glad you did not nurse him:
Though he does bear some signs of me, yet you
Have too much blood in him.

   *Her.*                    What is this? sport?

   *Leon.* Bear the boy hence; he shall not come about
    her;
Away with him! and let her sport herself          60
With that she's big with; for 't is Polixenes
Has made thee swell thus.

   *Her.*                    But I'd say he had not,
And I'll be sworn you would believe my saying,
Howe'er you lean to the nayward.

   *Leon.*                    You, my lords,
Look on her, mark her well; be but about
To say, "She is a goodly lady," and
The justice of your hearts will thereto add,
"'T is a pity she's not honest, honourable:"
Praise her but for this her without-door form,   *outward presence*
Which, on my faith, deserves high speech, and straight
The shrug, the hum, or ha, these petty brands          71
That calumny doth use; O, I am out,          *marks of infamy*
That mercy does, for calumny will sear
Virtue itself: these shrugs, these hums and ha's,

When you have said "she's goodly," come between,
Ere you can say "she's honest:" but be't known,
From him that has most cause to grieve it should be,
She's an adulteress.

   *Her.*            Should a villain say so,
The most replenish'd villain in the world,
He were as much more villain: you, my lord,     80
Do but mistake.

   *Leon.*      You have mistook, my lady,
Polixenes for Leontes: O thou thing!
Which I'll not call a creature of thy place,
Lest barbarism, making me the precedent,
Should a like language use to all degrees,
And mannerly distinguishment leave out
Betwixt the prince and beggar: I have said
She's an adulteress; I have said with whom:
More, she's a traitor and Camillo is
A federary with her; ay, and privy     90
To this their late escape.

   *Her.*            No, by my life,
Privy to none of this.   How will this grieve you,
When you shall come to clearer knowledge, that
You thus have publish'd me!   Gentle my lord,
You scarce can right me throughly then, to say
You did mistake.

   *Leon.*     No, if I mistake
In those foundations which I build upon,
The centre is not big enough to bear
A schoolboy's top.   Away with her, to prison!
He who will speak for her is afar off guilty     100
But that he speaks.

   *Her.*         There's some ill planet reigns:
I must be patient till the heavens look
With an aspéct more favourable.   Good my lords,
I am not prone to weeping, as our sex

Commonly are; the want of which vain dew
Perchance shall dry your pities; but I have
That honourable grief lodged here which burns
Worse than tears drown: beseech you all, my lords,
With thoughts so qualified as your charities
Shall best instruct you, measure me; and so          110
The king's will be performed!

    *Leon.*               Shall I be heard?

    *Her.* Who is 't that goes with me?   Beseech your
    highness,
My women may be with me; for, you see,
My plight requires it.   Do not weep, good fools;
There is no cause: when you shall know your mistress
Has deserv'd prison, then abound in tears
As I come out: this action I now go on
Is for my better grace.   Adieu, my lord:
I never wish'd to see you sorry; now
I trust I shall.   My women, come; you have leave. 120

    *Leon.* Go, do our bidding; hence!

               *[Exeunt Hermione, guarded, and Ladies.*

    *First Lord.* Beseech your highness, call the queen
    again.

    *Ant.* Be certain what you do, sir, lest your justice
Prove violence; in the which three great ones suffer,
Yourself, your queen, your son.

    *First Lord.*             For her, my lord,
I dare my life lay down, and will do 't, sir,
Please you to accept it, that the queen is spotless
I' the eyes of heaven and to you; I mean,
In this which you accuse her.

    *Ant.*                If it prove
She 's otherwise, I 'll keep my stables where          130
I lodge my wife; I 'll go in couples with her;
Than when I feel and see her no further trust her;
For every inch of woman in the world,

Ay, every dram of woman's flesh, is false,
If she be.
    *Leon.*    Hold your peaces.
    *First Lord.*                 Good my lord,—
    *Ant.*  It is for you we speak, not for ourselves:
You are abused, and by some putter-on
That will be damn'd for 't; would I knew the villain,
I would land-damn him.  Be she honour-flaw'd,—
I have three daughters; the eldest is eleven;    140
The second and the third, nine and some five;
If this prove true, they 'll pay for 't:
    *Leon.*               Cease; no more.
You smell this business with a sense as cold
As is a dead man's nose: But I do see 't and feel 't,
As you feel doing thus, and see withal
The instruments that feel.
    *Ant.*           If it be so,
We need no grave to bury honesty:
There 's not a grain of it the face to sweeten
Of the whole dungy earth.
    *Leon.*          What! lack I credit?
    *First Lord.*  I had rather you did lack than I, my lord,
Upon this ground; and more it would content me    151
To have her honour true than your suspicion,
Be blam'd for 't how you might.
    *Leon.*          Why, what need we
Commune with you of this, but rather follow
Our forceful instigation?  Our prerogative
Calls not your counsels; but our natural goodness
Imparts this: which, if you, or stupefied
Or seeming so in skill, cannot or will not
Relish a truth, like us, inform yourselves
We need no more of your advice: the matter,    160
The loss, the gain, the ordering on 't, is all
Properly ours.

*Ant.*            And I wish, my liege,
You had only in your silent judgment tried it,
Without more overture.
      *Leon.*                    How could that be?
Either thou art most ignorant by age,
Or thou wert born a fool.   Camillo's flight,
Added to their familiarity,
Which was as gross as ever touch'd conjecture,
That lack'd sight only, nought for approbation
But only seeing, all other circumstances            170
Made up to the deed,—doth push on this proceeding:
Yet, for a greater confirmation,
For, in an act of this importance 't were
Most piteous to be wild, I have dispatch'd in post
To sacred Delphos, to Apollo's temple,
Cleomenes and Dion, whom you know
Of stuff'd sufficiency: now, from the oracle
They will bring all; whose spiritual counsel had,
Shall stop or spur me.   Have I done well?
      *First Lord.* Well done, my lord.                180
      *Leon.* Though I am satisfied, and need no more
Than what I know, yet shall the oracle
Give rest to the minds of others, such as he
Whose ignorant credulity will not
Come up to the truth.   So have we thought it good
From our free person she should be confin'd,
Lest that the treachery of the two fled hence
Be left her to perform.   Come, follow us;
We are to speak in public; for this business
Will raise us all.
      *Ant.* [*Aside*] To laughter, as I take it,            190
If the good truth were known.                [*Exeunt.*

SCENE II.   *A prison*

*Enter* PAULINA, *a* Gentleman, *and* Attendants

*Paul.*  The keeper of the prison, call to him;
Let him have knowledge who I am.     [*Exit Gentleman.*
                                    Good lady,
No court in Europe is too good for thee;
What dost thou then in prison?

*Re-enter* Gentleman, *with the* Gaoler

                                    Now, good sir,
You know me, do you not?
    *Gaol.*                        For a worthy lady,
And one who much I honour.
    *Paul.*                        Pray you, then,
Conduct me to the queen.
    *Gaol.*                        I may not, madam:
To the contrary I have express commandment.
    *Paul.*  Here's ado,
To lock up honesty and honour from                    10
The access of gentle visitors!   Is't lawful, pray you,
To see her women? any of them? Emilia?
    *Gaol.*  So please you, madam,
To put apart these your attendants, I
Shall bring Emilia forth.
    *Paul.*                        I pray now, call her.
Withdraw yourselves.
                    [*Exeunt Gentleman and Attendants.*
    *Gaol.*                And, madam,
I must be present at your conference.
    *Paul.*  Well, be't so, prithee.     [*Exit Gaoler.*
Here's such ado to make no stain a stain
As passes colouring.

*Re-enter* Gaoler, *with* EMILIA

Dear gentlewoman,        20
How fares our gracious lady?

*Emil.* As well as one so great and so forlorn
May hold together: on her frights and griefs,
Which never tender lady hath borne greater,
She is, something before her time, deliver'd.

*Paul.* A boy?

*Emil.*        A daughter; and a goodly babe,
Lusty, and like to live: the queen receives
Much comfort in 't; says, " My poor prisoner,
I am innocent as you."

*Paul.*        I dare be sworn:
These dangerous unsafe lunes i' the king, beshrew them!
He must be told on 't, and he shall: the office        31
Becomes a woman best; I 'll take 't upon me:
If I prove honey-mouth'd, let my tongue blister,
And never to my red-look'd anger be
The trumpet any more.   Pray you, Emilia,
Commend my best obedience to the queen:
If she dares trust me with her little babe,
I 'll show 't the king, and undertake to be
Her advocate to the loud'st.   We do not know
How he may soften at the sight o' the child:        40
The silence often of pure innocence
Persuades when speaking fails.

*Emil.*        Most worthy madam,
Your honour and your goodness is so evident,
That your free undertaking cannot miss
A thriving issue: there 's no lady living
So meet for this great errand.   Please your ladyship
To visit the next room, I 'll presently
Acquaint the queen of your most noble offer;
Who but to-day hammered of this design,

But durst not tempt a minister of honour,          50
Lest she should be denied.

  *Paul.*      Tell her, Emilia,
I 'll use that tongue I have: if wit flow from 't,
As boldness from my bosom, let 't not be doubted
I shall do good.

  *Emil.*    Now be you bless'd for it!
I 'll to the queen: please you, come something nearer.

  *Gaol.* Madam, if 't please the queen to send the babe,
I know not what I shall incur to pass it,
Having no warrant.

  *Paul.*    You need not fear it, sir:
The child was prisoner to the womb, and is
By law and process of great nature thence          60
Freed and enfranchised; not a party to
The anger of the king, nor guilty of,
If any be, the trespass of the queen.

  *Gaol.* I do believe it.

  *Paul.* Do not you fear: upon mine honour, I
Will stand betwixt you and danger.   [*Exeunt.*

### Scene III.  *A room in Leontes' palace*

*Enter* LEONTES, ANTIGONUS, Lords, *and* Servants

  *Leon.* Nor night nor day no rest: it is but weakness
To bear the matter thus: mere weakness.   If
The cause were not in being,—part o' the cause,
She the adulteress; for the harlot king
Is quite beyond mine arm, out of the blank
And level of my brain, plot-proof; but she
I can hook to me: say that she were gone,
Given to the fire, a moiety of my rest
Might come to me again.—Who 's there?

  *First Serv.*      My lord?

  *Leon.* How does the boy?

*First Serv.*                    He took good rest to-night;
'T is hoped his sickness is discharged.                11
    *Leon.*  To see his nobleness!
Conceiving the dishonour of his mother,
He straight declin'd, droop'd, took it deeply,
Fasten'd and fix'd the shame on 't in himself,
Threw off his spirit, his appetite, his sleep,
And downright languish'd.   Leave me solely: go,
See how he fares. [*Exit Servant.*]  Fie, fie! no thought
    of him:
The very thought of my revenges that way
Recoil upon me: in himself too mighty,               20
And in his parties, his alliance; let him be,
Until a time may serve: for present vengeance,
Take it on her.   Camillo and Polixenes
Laugh at me, make their pastime at my sorrow:
They should not laugh, if I could reach them; nor
Shall she, within my power.

### *Enter* PAULINA, *with a* Child

*First Lord.*                    You must not enter.
    *Paul.*  Nay, rather, good my lords, be second to me:
Fear you his tyrannous passion more, alas,
Than the queen's life? a gracious innocent soul,
More free than he is jealous.
    *Ant.*                    That 's enough.       30
    *Sec. Atten.*  Madam, he hath not slept to-night; com-
    manded
None should come at him.
    *Paul.*                    Not so hot, good sir:
I come to bring him sleep.   'T is such as you,
That creep like shadows by him, and do sigh
At each his needless heavings, such as you
Nourish the cause of his awaking: I
Do come with words as medicinal as true,

Honest as either, to purge him of that humour
That presses him from sleep.
    *Leon.*           What noise there, ho?
    *Paul.*  No noise, my lord; but needful conference   40
About some gossips for your highness.
    *Leon.*           How!
Away with that audacious lady! Antigonus,
I charged thee that she should not come about me:
I knew she would.
    *Ant.*        I told her so, my lord,
On your displeasure's peril and on mine,
She should not visit you.
    *Leon.*        What, canst not rule her?
    *Paul.*  From all dishonesty he can: in this,
Unless he take the course that you have done,
Commit me for committing honour, trust it,
He shall not rule me.
    *Ant.*      La you now, you hear:   50
When she will take the rein, I let her run;
But she'll not stumble.
    *Paul.*      Good my liege, I come;
And, I beseech you, hear me, who professes
Myself your loyal servant, your physician,
Your most obedient councillor, yet that dares
Less appear so in comforting your evils,
Than such as most seem yours: I say, I come
From your good queen.
    *Leon.*      Good queen!
    *Paul.*      Good queen, my lord,
Good queen; I say good queen;
And would by combat make her good, so were I   60
A man, the worst about you.
    *Leon.*      Force her hence.
    *Paul.*  Let him that makes but trifles of his eyes
First hand me: on mine own accord I'll off;

But first I 'll do my errand.   The good queen,
For she is good, hath brought you forth a daughter;
Here 't is; commends it to your blessing.

> [*Lays down the Child.*

   *Leon.*                                        Out!
A mankind witch!   Hence with her, out o' door:
A most intelligencing bawd!
   *Paul.*                          Not so:
I am as ignorant in that as you
In so entitling me, and no less honest          70
Than you are mad; which is enough, I 'll warrant,
As this world goes, to pass for honest.
   *Leon.*                                      Traitors!
Will you not push her out?   Give her the bastard;
[*To Antigonus*]   Thou dotard, thou art woman-tir'd,
    unroosted
By thy dame Partlet here.   Take up the bastard;
Take 't up, I say; give 't to thy crone.
   *Paul.*                              For ever
Unvenerable be thy hands, if thou
Tak'st up the princess by that forced baseness
Which he has put upon 't!
   *Leon.*                      He dreads his wife.     79
   *Paul.*   So I would you did; then 't were past all doubt
You'd call your children yours.
   *Leon.*                          A nest of traitors!
   *Ant.*   I am none, by this good light.
   *Paul.*                          Nor I; nor any,
But one that 's here, and that 's himself; for he
The sacred honour of himself, his queen's,
His hopeful son's, his babe's, betrays to slander,
Whose sting is sharper than the sword's; and will not—
For, as the case now stands, it is a curse
He cannot be compell'd to 't—once remove
The root of his opinion, which is rotten

As ever oak or stone was sound.

    *Leon.*               A callat     90
Of boundless tongue, who late hath beat her husband,
And now baits me! This brat is none of mine;
It is the issue of Polixenes:
Hence with it; and together with the dam
Commit them to the fire!

    *Paul.*            It is yours;
And, might we lay the old proverb to your charge,
So, like you, 't is the worse.   Behold, my lords,
Although the print be little, the whole matter
And copy of the father, eye, nose, lip;
The trick of 's frown; his forehead; nay, the valley,   100
The pretty dimples of his chin and cheek; his smiles;
The very mould and frame of hand, nail, finger:
And thou, good goddess Nature, which hast made it
So like to him that got it, if thou hast
The ordering of the mind too, 'mongst all colours
No yellow in 't, lest she suspect, as he does,
Her children not her husband's!

    *Leon.*           A gross hag!
And, lozel, thou art worthy to be hang'd,
That wilt not stay her tongue.

    *Ant.*          Hang all the husbands
That cannot do that feat, you 'll leave yourself   110
Hardly one subject.

    *Leon.*       Once more, take her hence.

    *Paul.* A most unworthy and unnatural lord
Can do no more.

    *Leon.*     I 'll ha' thee burnt.

    *Paul.*            I care not:
It is an heretic that makes the fire,
Not she which burns in 't.   I 'll not call you tyrant;
But this most cruel usage of your queen—
Not able to produce more accusation

Than your own weak-hing'd fancy—something savours
Of tyranny, and will ignoble make you,
Yea, scandalous to the world.

*Leon.*                    On your allegiance,  120
Out of the chamber with her!   Were I a tyrant,
Where were her life? she durst not call me so,
If she did know me one.   Away with her!

*Paul.* I pray you, do not push me; I'll be gone.
Look to your babe, my lord; 'tis yours: Jove send her
A better guiding spirit!   What needs these hands?
You, that are thus so tender o'er his follies,
Will never do him good, not one of you.
So, so: farewell; we are gone.          [*Exit.*

*Leon.* Thou, traitor, hast set on thy wife to this.  130
My child? away with it!   Even thou, that hast
A heart so tender o'er it, take it hence
And see it instantly consum'd with fire;
Even thou and none but thou.   Take it up straight:
Within this hour bring me word 'tis done,
And by good testimony, or I'll seize thy life,
With what thou else call'st thine.   If thou refuse,
And wilt encounter with my wrath, say so;
The bastard-brains with these my proper hands
Shall I dash out.   Go, take it to the fire;          140
For thou sett'st on thy wife.

*Ant.*                    I did not, sir:
These lords, my noble fellows, if they please,
Can clear me in 't.

*First Lord.*      We can: my royal liege,
He is not guilty of her coming hither.

*Leon.* You're liars all.

*First Lord.* Beseech your highness, give us better
     credit:
We have always truly serv'd you; and beseech you
So to esteem of us: and on our knees we beg,

As recompense of our dear services
Past and to come, that you do change this purpose, 150
Which being so horrible, so bloody, must
Lead on to some foul issue: we all kneel.

   *Leon.* I am a feather for each wind that blows:
Shall I live on, to see this bastard kneel
And call me father? better burn it now
Than curse it then. But be it; let it live.
It shall not neither. You, sir, come you hither;
You that have been so tenderly officious
With Lady Margery, your midwife there,
To save this bastard's life,—for 't is a bastard,     160
So sure as this beard's gray,—what will you adventure
To save this brat's life?

   *Ant.*              Any thing, my lord,
That my ability may undergo,
And nobleness impose: at least, thus much:
I'll pawn the little blood which I have left
To save the innocent: any thing possible.

   *Leon.* It shall be possible. Swear by this sword
Thou wilt perform my bidding.

   *Ant.*              I will, my lord.

   *Leon.* Mark, and perform it: seest thou? for the fail
Of any point in 't shall not only be     170
Death to thyself, but to thy lewd-tongued wife,
Whom for this time we pardon. We enjoin thee,
As thou art liegeman to us, that thou carry
This female bastard hence, and that thou bear it
To some remote and desert place, quite out
Of our dominions, and that there thou leave it,
Without more mercy, to its own protection
And favour of the climate. As by strange fortune
It came to us, I do in justice charge thee,
On thy soul's peril and thy body's torture,     180
That thou commend it strangely to some place

Where chance may nurse or end it.   Take it up.
   *Ant.* I swear to do this, though a present death
Had been more merciful.   Come on, poor babe:
Some powerful spirit instruct the kites and ravens
To be thy nurses! Wolves and bears, they say,
Casting their savageness aside, have done
Like offices of pity.   Sir, be prosperous
In more than this deed does require!   And blessing
Against this cruelty fight on thy side,        190
Poor thing condemn'd to loss!   [*Exit with the Child.*
   *Leon.*                No, I'll not rear
Another's issue.

### Enter a Servant

   *Serv.*       Please your highness, posts
From those you sent to the oracle are come
An hour since: Cleomenes and Dion,
Being well arriv'd from Delphos, are both landed,
Hasting to the court.
   *First Lord.*      So please you, sir, their speed
Hath been beyond account.
   *Leon.*               Twenty-three days
They have been absent: 't is good speed; foretells
The great Apollo suddenly will have
The truth of this appear.   Prepare you, lords;   200
Summon a session, that we may arraign
Our most disloyal lady; for, as she hath
Been publicly accus'd, so shall she have
A just and open trial.   While she lives
My heart will be a burden to me.   Leave me,
And think upon my bidding.            [*Exeunt.*

# ACT III

## SCENE I.  *A town in Sicilia*

### *Enter* CLEOMENES *and* DION, *attended*

*Cleo.* The climate's delicate, the air most sweet,
Fertile the isle, the temple much surpassing
The common praise it bears.

*Dion.*                    I shall report,
For most it caught me, the celestial habits,
Methinks I so should term them, and the reverence
Of the grave wearers.  O, the sacrifice;
How ceremonious, solemn, and unearthly
It was i' the offering!

*Cleo.*                        But of all, the burst
And the ear-deafening voice o' the oracle,
Kin to Jove's thunder, so surpris'd my sense,                10
That I was nothing.

*Dion.*                        If the event o' the journey
Prove as successful to the queen,—O be 't so!—
As it hath been to us rare, pleasant, speedy,
The time is worth the use on 't.

*Cleo.*                              Great Apollo
Turn all to the best!  These proclamations,
So forcing faults upon Hermione,
I little like.

*Dion.*      The violent carriage of it
Will clear or end the business: when the oracle,
Thus by Apollo's great divine sealed up,
Shall the contents discover, something rare          20
Even then will rush to knowledge.  Go: fresh horses!
And gracious be the issue!                    [*Exeunt.*

SCENE II.  *A court of justice*

*Enter* LEONTES, *Lords, and* Officers

*Leon.* This sessions, to our great grief we pronounce,
Even pushes 'gainst our heart: the party tried,
The daughter of a king, our wife, and one
Of us too much belov'd.   Let us be clear'd
Of being tyrannous, since we so openly
Proceed in justice, which shall have due course,
Even to the guilt or the purgation.
Produce the prisoner.

*Offi.* It is his highness' pleasure that the queen
Appear in person here in court.   Silence!          10

*Enter* HERMIONE, *guarded;* PAULINA *and*
Ladies *attending*

*Leon.* Read the indictment.

*Offi.* [*Reads*] "Hermione, queen to the worthy Leontes, king
of Sicilia, thou art here accused and arraigned of high treason, in
committing adultery with Polixenes, king of Bohemia, and conspiring with Camillo to take away the life of our sovereign lord the
king, thy royal husband: the pretence whereof being by circumstances partly laid open, thou, Hermione, contrary to the faith and
allegiance of a true subject, didst counsel and aid them, for their
better safety, to fly away by night."

*Her.* Since what I am to say must be but that          20
Which contradicts my accusation and
The testimony on my part no other
But what comes from myself, it shall scarce boot me
To say, "Not guilty:" mine integrity
Being counted falsehood, shall, as I express it,
Be so receiv'd.   But thus, if powers divine
Behold our human actions, as they do,
I doubt not then but innocence shall make
False accusation blush, and tyranny

Tremble at patience.   You, my lord, best know,        30
Who least will seem to do so, my past life
Hath been as continent, as chaste, as true,
As I am now unhappy; which is more
Than history can pattern, though devis'd
And play'd to take spectators.   For behold me,
A fellow of the royal bed, which owe
A moiety of the throne, a great king's daughter,
The mother to a hopeful prince, here standing
To prate and talk for life and honour 'fore
Who please to come and hear.   For life, I prize it     40
As I weigh grief, which I would spare: for honour,
'T is a derivative from me to mine,
And only that I stand for.   I appeal
To your own conscience, sir, before Polixenes
Came to your court, how I was in your grace,
How merited to be so; since he came,
With what encounter so uncurrent I
Have strain'd, to appear thus: if one jot beyond
The bound of honour, or in act or will
That way inclining, harden'd be the hearts        50
Of all that hear me, and my near'st of kin
Cry fie upon my grave!
     *Leon.*              I ne'er heard yet
That any of these bolder vices wanted
Less impudence to gainsay what they did
Than to perform it first.
     *Her.*              That 's true enough;
Though 't is a saying, sir, not due to me.
     *Leon.* You will not own it.
     *Her.*              More than mistress of
Which comes to me in name of fault, I must not
At all acknowledge.   For Polixenes,
With whom I am accus'd, I do confess        60
I lov'd him as in honour he requir'd,

With such a kind of love as might become
A lady like me, with a love even such,
So and no other, as yourself commanded:
Which not to have done, I think had been in me
Both disobedience and ingratitude
To you and toward your friend; whose love had spoke,
Even since it could speak, from an infant, freely,
That it was yours.  Now, for conspiracy,
I know not how it tastes; though it be dish'd          70
For me to try how: all I know of it
Is that Camillo was an honest man;
And why he left your court, the gods themselves,
Wotting no more than I, are ignorant.

   *Leon.*  You knew of his departure, as you know what
You 've underta'en to do in 's absence.

   *Her.*                                    Sir,
You speak a language that I understand not:
My life stands in the level of your dreams,
Which I' ll lay down.

   *Leon.*                    Your actions are my dreams;
You had a bastard by Polixenes,          80
And I but dream'd it.  As you were past all shame,—
Those of your fact are so,—so past all truth:
Which to deny concerns more than avails; for as
Thy brat hath been cast out, like to itself,
No father owning it,—which is, indeed,
More criminal in thee than it,—so thou
Shalt feel our justice; in whose easiest passage
Look for no less than death.

   *Her.*                        Sir, spare your threats:
The bug which you would fright me with I seek.
To me can life be no commodity:          90
The crown and comfort of my life, your favour,
I do give lost; for I do feel it gone,
But know not how it went.  My second joy

And first-fruits of my body, from his presence
I am barr'd, like one infectious.   My third comfort,
Starr'd most unluckily, is from my breast,
The innocent milk in its most innocent mouth,
Haled out to murder: myself on every post
Proclaim'd a strumpet; with immodest hatred
The child-bed privilege denied, which 'longs           100
To women of all fashion; lastly, hurried
Here to this place, i' the open air, before
I have got strength of limit.   Now, my liege,
Tell me what blessings I have here alive,
That I should fear to die?   Therefore proceed.
But yet hear this; mistake me not; no life,
I prize it not a straw, but for mine honour,
Which I would free, if I shall be condemn'd
Upon surmises, all proofs sleeping else
But what your jealousies awake, I tell you,             110
'T is rigour, and not law.   Your honours all,
I do refer me to the oracle:
Apollo be my judge!
    *First Lord.*        This your request
Is altogether just: therefore, bring forth,
And in Apollo's name, his oracle. [*Exeunt some Officers.*
    *Her.* The emperor of Russia was my father:
O that he were alive, and here beholding
His daughter's trial! that he did but see
The flatness of my misery, yet with eyes
Of pity, not revenge!                                   120

    *Re-enter* Officers, *with* CLEOMENES *and* DION

    *First Offi.* You here shall swear upon this sword of
        justice,
That you, Cleomenes and Dion, have
Been both at Delphos, and from thence have brought
This seal'd-up oracle, by the hand deliver'd
    3                                        (D 656)

Of great Apollo's priest; and that since then
You have not dar'd to break the holy seal
Nor read the secrets in 't.

    *Cleo. Dion.*          All this we swear.

    *Leon.* Break up the seals and read.

    *Offi.* [*Reads*] "Hermione is chaste; Polixenes blameless;
Camillo a true subject; Leontes a jealous tyrant; his innocent
babe truly begotten; and the king shall live without an heir, if
that which is lost be not found."          132

    *Lords.* Now blessed be the great Apollo!

    *Her.*                    Praised!

    *Leon.* Hast thou read truth?

    *First Offi.*          Ay, my lord; even so
As it is here set down.

    *Leon.* There is no truth at all i' the oracle:
The sessions shall proceed: this is mere falsehood.

*A* Servant *rushes in*

    *Serv.* My lord the king, the king!

    *Leon.*              What is the business?

    *Serv.* O sir, I shall be hated to report it!
The prince your son, with mere conceit and fear    140
Of the queen's speed, is gone.

    *Leon.*          How? gone?

    *Serv.*                  Is dead.

    *Leon.* Apollo's angry; and the heavens themselves
Do strike at my injustice. [*Hermione swoons.*] How
    now there!

    *Paul.* This news is mortal to the queen: look down,
And see what death is doing.

    *Leon.*             Take her hence:
Her heart is but o'ercharg'd; she will recover:
I have too much believ'd mine own suspicion:
Beseech you, tenderly apply to her

Some remedies for life.

[*Exeunt Paulina and Ladies, with Hermione.*

Apollo, pardon
My great profaneness 'gainst thine oracle!—          150
I 'll reconcile me to Polixenes,
New woo my queen, recall the good Camillo,
Whom I proclaim a man of truth, of mercy;
For, being transported by my jealousies
To bloody thoughts and to revenge, I chose
Camillo for the minister, to poison
My friend Polixenes: which had been done,
But that the good mind of Camillo tardied
My swift command, though I with death and with
Reward did threaten and encourage him,          160
Not doing it and being done: he, most humane,
And fill'd with honour, to my kingly guest
Unclasp'd my practice, quit his fortunes here,
Which you knew great, and to the hazard
Of all incertainties himself commended,
No richer than his honour: how he glisters
Through my rust! and how his piety
Does my deeds make the blacker!

*Re-enter* PAULINA

*Paul.*                         Woe the while!
O, cut my lace, lest my heart, cracking it,
Break too!
    *First Lord.* What fit is this, good lady?          170
    *Paul.* What studied torments, tyrant, hast for me?
What wheels? racks? fires? what flaying? boiling
In leads or oils? what old or newer torture
Must I receive, whose every word deserves
To taste of thy most worst?   Thy tyranny
Together working with thy jealousies,—
Fancies too weak for boys, too green and idle

For girls of nine,—O, think what they have done,
And then run mad indeed, stark mad! for all
Thy by-gone fooleries were but spices of it.          180
That thou betray'dst Polixenes, 't was nothing;
That did but show thee, of a fool, inconstant
And damnable ingrateful: nor was 't much,
Thou wouldst have poison'd good Camillo's honour,
To have him kill a king; poor trespasses,
More monstrous standing by: whereof I reckon
The casting forth to crows thy baby daughter,
To be or none or little; though a devil
Would have shed water out of fire ere done 't:
Nor is 't directly laid to thee, the death          190
Of the young prince, whose honourable thoughts,
Thoughts high for one so tender, cleft the heart
That could conceive a gross and foolish sire
Blemish'd his gracious dam: this is not, no,
Laid to thy answer: but the last,—O lords,
When I have said, cry "woe!"—the queen, the queen,
The sweet'st, dear'st creature's dead; and vengeance
     for 't
Not dropp'd down yet.
     *First Lord.*          The higher powers forbid!
     *Paul.* I say she's dead; I'll swear 't.   If word nor
     oath
Prevail not, go and see: if you can bring          200
Tincture or lustre in her lip, her eye,
Heat outwardly or breath within, I'll serve you
As I would do the gods.   But, O thou tyrant!
Do not repent these things, for they are heavier
Than all thy woes can stir: therefore betake thee
To nothing but despair.   A thousand knees
Ten thousand years together, naked, fasting,
Upon a barren mountain, and still winter
In storm perpetual, could not move the gods

To look that way thou wert.
    *Leon.*               Go on, go on:     210
Thou canst not speak too much; I have deserv'd
All tongues to talk their bitterest.
    *First Lord.*          Say no more:
Howe'er the business goes, you have made fault
I' the boldness of your speech.
    *Paul.*           I am sorry for 't:
All faults I make, when I shall come to know them,
I do repent.   Alas, I have show'd too much
The rashness of a woman! he is touch'd
To the noble heart.   What 's gone and what 's past help
Should be past grief: do not receive affliction
At my petition; I beseech you, rather     220
Let me be punish'd, that have minded you
Of what you should forget.   Now, good my liege,
Sir, royal sir, forgive a foolish woman:
The love I bore your queen,—lo, fool again!
I 'll speak of her no more, nor of your children;
I 'll not remember you of my own lord,
Who is lost too: take your patience to you,
And I 'll say nothing.
    *Leon.*        Thou didst speak but well,
When most the truth; which I receive much better
Than to be pitied of thee.   Prithee, bring me     230
To the dead bodies of my queen and son:
One grave shall be for both; upon them shall
The causes of their death appear, unto
Our shame perpetual.   Once a day I 'll visit
The chapel where they lie, and tears shed there
Shall be my recreation: so long as nature
Will bear up with this exercise, so long
I daily vow to use it.   Come, and lead me
To these sorrows.                 [*Exeunt.*

SCENE III.    *Bohemia.    A desert country near the sea*

*Enter* ANTIGONUS *with the* Child, *and a* Mariner

*Ant.* Thou art perfect, then, our ship hath touch'd
    upon
The deserts of Bohemia?
    *Mar.*                    Ay, my lord; and fear
We have landed in ill time: the skies look grimly,
And threaten present blusters.    In my conscience,
The heavens with that we have in hand are angry
And frown upon 's.
    *Ant.* Their sacred wills be done!    Go, get aboard;
Look to thy bark: I 'll not be long before
I call upon thee.
    *Mar.* Make your best haste; and go not          10
Too far i' the land: 't is like to be loud weather;
Besides, this place is famous for the creatures
Of prey that keep upon 't.
    *Ant.*                    Go thou away:
I 'll follow instantly.
    *Mar.*                I am glad at heart
To be so rid o' the business.                    [*Exit.*
    *Ant.*                    Come, poor babe:
I have heard, but not believ'd, the spirits o' the dead
May walk again: if such thing be, thy mother
Appear'd to me last night, for ne'er was dream
So like a waking.    To me comes a creature,
Sometimes her head on one side, some another;          20
I never saw a vessel of like sorrow
So fill'd and so becoming: in pure white robes,
Like very sanctity, she did approach
My cabin where I lay; thrice bow'd before me,
And gasping to begin some speech, her eyes
Became two spouts: the fury spent, anon

Did this break from her: "Good Antigonus,
Since fate, against thy better disposition,
Hath made thy person for the thrower-out
Of my poor babe, according to thine oath,          30
Places remote enough are in Bohemia,
There weep, and leave it crying; and, for the babe
Is counted lost for ever, Perdita,
I prithee, call 't.   For this ungentle business,
Put on thee by my lord, thou ne'er shalt see
Thy wife Paulina more."   And so, with shrieks,
She melted into air.   Affrighted much,
I did in time collect myself, and thought
This was so, and no slumber.   Dreams are toys.
Yet, for this once, yea, superstitiously,          40
I will be squar'd by this.   I do believe
Hermione hath suffer'd death; and that
Apollo would, this being indeed the issue
Of king Polixenes, it should here be laid,
Either for life or death, upon the earth
Of its right father.   Blossom, speed thee well!
There lie, and there thy character: there these;
Which may, if fortune please, both breed thee, pretty,
And still rest thine.   The storm begins: poor wretch,
That, for thy mother's fault art thus expos'd          50
To loss and what may follow!   Weep I cannot,
But my heart bleeds; and most accurs'd am I
To be by oath enjoin'd to this.   Farewell!
The day frowns more and more: thou 'rt like to have
A lullaby too rough: I never saw
The heavens so dim by day.   A savage clamour!
Well may I get aboard!   This is the chase:          57
I am gone for ever!          [*Exit pursued by a bear.*

*Enter a* Shepherd

*Shep.* I would there were no age between ten and

three-and-twenty, or that youth would sleep out the
rest; for there is nothing in the between but wronging
the ancientry, stealing, fighting— Hark you now!
Would any but these boiled brains of nineteen and two-
and-twenty hunt this weather? They have scar'd away
two of my best sheep, which I fear the wolf will sooner
find than the master: if any where I have them, 't is by
the sea-side, browsing of ivy. Good luck, an 't be thy
will! what have we here? Mercy on 's, a barne; a very
pretty barne! A boy or a child, I wonder! A pretty
one; a very pretty one: sure, some scape: though I am
not bookish, yet I can read waiting-gentlewoman in
the scape. This has been some stair-work, some trunk-
work, some behind-door-work. I 'll take it up for pity:
yet I 'll tarry till my son come; he halloo'd but even now.
Whoa, ho, hoa!                                                          75

Enter Clown

*Clo.* Hilloa, loa!

*Shep.* What, art so near! If thou'lt see a thing to
talk on when thou art dead and rotten, come hither.
What ailest thou, man?

*Clo.* I have seen two such sights, by sea and by land!
but I am not to say it is a sea, for it is now the sky:
betwixt the firmament and it you cannot thrust a bod-
kin's point.                                                              83

*Shep.* Why, boy, how is it?

*Clo.* I would you did but see how it chafes, how it
rages, how it takes up the shore! but that's not to the
point. O, the most piteous cry of the poor souls!
sometimes to see 'em, and not to see 'em; now the ship
boring the moon with her main-mast, and anon swallowed with yest and froth, as you 'd thrust a cork into
a hogshed. And then for the land-service, to see how
the bear tore out his shoulder-bone; how he cried to me
for help, and said his name was Antigonus, a nobleman.

But to make an end of the ship, to see how the sea flap-
dragon'd it: but, first, how the poor souls roared, and the
sea mock'd them; and how the poor gentleman roared,
and the bear mock'd him, both roaring louder than the
sea or weather.                                              98

*Shep.* Name of mercy, when was this, boy?

*Clo.* Now, now: I have not wink'd since I saw these
sights: the men are not yet cold under water, nor the
bear half din'd on the gentleman: he 's at it now.

*Shep.* Would I had been by, to have help'd the old
man!

*Clo.* I would you had been by the ship-side, to have
help'd her: there your charity would have lack'd footing.

*Shep.* Heavy matters! heavy matters! but look thee
here, boy.    Now bless thyself: thou mettest with things
dying, I with things newborn.   Here 's a sight for thee;
look thee, a bearing-cloth for a squire's child!  look
thee here; take up, take up, boy; open 't.  So, let 's see:
it was told me I should be rich by the fairies.   This is
some changeling: open 't.   What 's within, boy?   113

*Clo.* You 're a made old man: if the sins of your
youth are forgiven you, you 're well to live.   Gold! all
gold!

*Shep.* This is fairy gold, boy, and 't will prove so:
up with 't, keep it close: home, home, the next way.
We are lucky, boy; and to be so still, requires nothing
but secrecy.   Let my sheep go: come, good boy, the
next way home.                                             121

*Clo.* Go you the next way with your findings.   I 'll go
see if the bear be gone from the gentleman, and how
much he hath eaten: they are never curst, but when
they are hungry: if there be any of him left, I 'll bury it.

*Shep.* That 's a good deed.   If thou mayest discern
by that which is left of him what he is, fetch me to the
sight of him.

3●

*Clo.* Marry, will I; and you shall help to put him i'
the ground.                                              130

*Shep.* 'T is a lucky day, boy, and we 'll do good deeds
on 't.                                                  [*Exeunt.*

---

## ACT IV

### SCENE I

*Enter* TIME, *the* Chorus

*Time.* I, that please some, try all, both joy and terror
Of good and bad, that makes and unfolds error,
Now take upon me, in the name of Time,
To use my wings.   Impute it not a crime
To me or my swift passage, that I slide
O'er sixteen years, and leave the growth untried
Of that wide gap, since it is in my power
To o'erthrow law and in one self-born hour
To plant and o'erwhelm custom.   Let me pass
The same I am, ere ancient'st order was            10
Or what is now receiv'd: I witness to
The times that brought them in; so shall I do
To the freshest things now reigning, and make stale
The glistering of this present, as my tale
Now seems to it.   Your patience this allowing,
I turn my glass, and give my scene such growing
As you had slept between: Leontes leaving,
The effects of his fond jealousies so grieving
That he shuts up himself, imagine me,
Gentle spectators, that I now may be              20
In fair Bohemia; and remember well,
I mentioned a son o' the king's, which Florizel
I now name to you; and with speed so pace
To speak of Perdita, now grown in grace

Equal with wondering: what of her ensues,
I list not prophesy; but let Time's news
Be known when 't is brought forth.   A shepherd's
      daughter,
And what to her adheres, which follows after,
Is the argument of Time.   Of this allow,
If ever you have spent time worse ere now;            30
If never, yet that Time himself doth say
He wishes earnestly you never may.            [*Exit.*

SCENE II.   *Bohemia.   The palace of Polixenes*

*Enter* POLIXENES *and* CAMILLO

*Pol.* I pray thee, good Camillo, be no more impor-
tunate: 't is a sickness denying thee any thing; a death
to grant this.

*Cam.* It is fifteen years since I saw my country:
though I have for the most part been aired abroad, I
desire to lay my bones there.   Besides, the penitent
king, my master, hath sent for me; to whose feeling
sorrows I might be some allay, or I o'erween to think
so, which is another spur to my departure.            9

*Pol.* As thou lovest me, Camillo, wipe not out the rest
of thy services by leaving me now; the need I have of
thee, thine own goodness hath made; better not to have
had thee than thus to want thee: thou, having made me
businesses which none without thee can sufficiently
manage, must either stay to execute them thyself, or
take away with thee the very services thou hast done;
which if I have not enough considered, as too much I
cannot, to be more thankful to thee shall be my study;
and my profit therein, the heaping friendships.   Of that
fatal country, Sicilia, prithee speak no more; whose
very naming punishes me with the remembrance of that
penitent, as thou callest him, and reconciled king, my

brother; whose loss of his most precious queen and children are even now to be afresh lamented. Say to me, when sawest thou the Prince Florizel, my son? Kings are no less unhappy, their issue not being gracious, than they are in losing them when they have approved their virtues.                                    28

*Cam.* Sir, it is three days since I saw the prince. What his happier affairs may be, are to me unknown; but I have missingly noted, he is of late much retired from court, and is less frequent to his princely exercises than formerly he hath appeared.

*Pol.* I have considered so much, Camillo, and with some care; so far, that I have eyes under my service which look upon his removedness; from whom I have this intelligence, that he is seldom from the house of a most homely shepherd; a man, they say, that from very nothing, and beyond the imagination of his neighbours, is grown into an unspeakable estate.                    40

*Cam.* I have heard, sir, of such a man, who hath a daughter of most rare note: the report of her is extended more than can be thought to begin from such a cottage.

*Pol.* That's likewise part of my intelligence; but, I fear, the angle that plucks our son thither. Thou shalt accompany us to the place; where we will, not appearing what we are, have some question with the shepherd; from whose simplicity I think it not uneasy to get the cause of my son's resort thither. Prithee, be my present partner in this business, and lay aside the thoughts of Sicilia.                                    52

*Cam.* I willingly obey your command.

*Pol.* My best Camillo! We must disguise ourselves.
                                          [*Exeunt.*

SCENE III.   *A road near the Shepherd's cottage*

*Enter* AUTOLYCUS, *singing*

When daffodils begin to peer,
    With, heigh! the doxy over the dale,
Why, then comes in the sweet o' the year;
    For the red blood reigns in the winter's pale.

The white sheet bleaching on the hedge,
    With, heigh! the sweet birds, O how they sing!
Doth set my pugging tooth on edge;
    For a quart of ale is a dish for a king.

The lark, that tirra-lirra chants,
    With, heigh! with, heigh! the thrush and the jay,          10
Are summer songs for me and my aunts,
    While we lie tumbling in the hay.

I have serv'd Prince Florizel and in my time wore three-
pile; but now I am out of service:

But shall I go mourn for that, my dear?
    The pale moon shines by night:
And when I wander here and there,
    I then do most go right.

If tinkers may have leave to live,
    And bear the sow-skin budget,                              20
Then my account I well may give,
    And in the stocks avouch it.

My traffic is sheets; when the kite builds, look to lesser
linen. My father nam'd me Autolycus; who being, as
I am, litter'd under Mercury, was likewise a snapper-up
of unconsidered trifles. With die and drab I purchas'd
this caparison; and my revenue is the silly cheat.
Gallows and knock are too powerful on the highway;
beating and hanging are terrors to me; for the life to
come, I sleep out the thought of it.  A prize! a prize!

*Enter* Clown

*Clo.* Let me see: every 'leven wether tods; every tod yields pound and odd shilling: fifteen hundred shorn, what comes the wool to?        33

*Aut.* [*Aside*] If the springe hold, the cock 's mine.

*Clo.* I cannot do 't without counters. Let me see; what am I to buy for our sheap-shearing feast? Three pound of sugar; five pound of currants; rice—what will this sister of mine do with rice? But my father hath made her mistress of the feast, and she lays it on. She hath made me four-and-twenty nosegays for the shearers, three-man songmen all, and very good ones; but they are most of them means and bases; but one puritan amongst them, and he sings psalms to hornpipes. I must have saffron, to colour the warden-pies; mace; dates, none, that 's out of my note; nut-megs, seven; a race or two of ginger, but that I may beg; four pound of prunes, and as many of raisins o' the sun.

*Aut.* O that ever I was born!

                                    [*Grovels on the ground.*

*Clo.* I' the name of me!        50

*Aut.* O, help me, help me! pluck but off these rags; and then, death, death!

*Clo.* Alack, poor soul! thou hast need of more rags to lay on thee, rather than have these off.

*Aut.* O, sir, the loathsomeness of them offend me more than the stripes I have received, which are mighty ones and millions.

*Clo.* Alas, poor man! a million of beating may come to a great matter.        59

*Aut.* I am robb'd, sir, and beaten; my money and apparel ta'en from me, and these detestable things put upon me.

*Clo.* What, by a horseman or a footman?

*Aut.* A footman, sweet sir, a footman.

*Clo.* Indeed, he should be a footman by the garments he has left with thee: if this be a horseman's coat, it hath seen very hot service. Lend me thy hand, I'll help thee: come, lend me thy hand.

*Aut.* O, good sir, tenderly, O!

*Clo.* Alas, poor soul! 70

*Aut.* O, good sir, softly, good sir! I fear, sir, my shoulder-blade is out.

*Clo.* How now! canst stand?

*Aut.* Softly, dear sir [*picks his pocket*]; good sir, softly. You ha' done me a charitable office.

*Clo.* Dost lack any money? I have a little money for thee.

*Aut.* No, good sweet sir; no, I beseech you, sir: I have a kinsman not past three-quarters of a mile hence, unto whom I was going; I shall there have money, or any thing I want: offer me no money, I pray you; that kills my heart. 82

*Clo.* What manner of fellow was he that robb'd you?

*Aut.* A fellow, sir, that I have known to go about with troll-my-dames: I knew him once a servant of the prince: I cannot tell, good sir, for which of his virtues it was, but he was certainly whipp'd out of the court.

*Clo.* His vices, you would say; there's no virtue whipp'd out of the court: they cherish it, to make it stay there; and yet it will no more but abide. 90

*Aut.* Vices, I would say, sir. I know this man well: he hath been since an ape-bearer; then a process-server, a bailiff; then he compass'd a motion of the Prodigal Son, and married a tinker's wife within a mile where my land and living lies; and, having flown over many knavish professions, he settled only in rogue: some call him Autolycus.

*Clo.* Out upon him! prig, for my life, prig: he haunts
wakes, fairs and bear-baitings.                              99

*Aut.* Very true, sir; he, sir, he; that's the rogue that
put me into this apparel.

*Clo.* Not a more cowardly rogue in all Bohemia; if
you had but look'd big and spit at him, he'd have run.

*Aut.* I must confess to you, sir, I am no fighter: I
am false of heart that way; and that he knew, I warrant
him.

*Clo.* How do you now?

*Aut.* Sweet sir, much better than I was; I can stand
and walk: I will even take my leave of you, and pace
softly towards my kinsman's.                                110

*Clo.* Shall I bring thee on the way?

*Aut.* No, good-fac'd sir; no, sweet sir.

*Clo.* Then fare thee well: I must go buy spices for
our sheep-shearing.

*Aut.* Prosper you, sweet sir! [*Exit Clown.*] Your
purse is not hot enough to purchase your spice. I'll be
with you at your sheep-shearing too: if I make not this
cheat bring out another, and the shearers prove sheep,
let me be unroll'd, and my name put in the book of
virtue!                                                      120

    Jog on, jog on, the footpath way,        [*Sings.*
      And merrily hent the stile-a:
    A merry heart goes all the day
      Your sad tires in a mile-a.             [*Exit.*

SCENE IV.  *The Shepherd's cottage*

*Enter* FLORIZEL *and* PERDITA

*Flo.* These your unusual weeds to each part of you
Do give a life: no shepherdess, but Flora
Peering in April's front. This your sheep-shearing
Is as a meeting of the petty gods,
And you the queen on't.

 *Per.*     Sir, my gracious lord,
To chide at your extremes, it not becomes me:
O, pardon that I name them!  Your high self,
The gracious mark o' the land, you have obscur'd
With a swain's wearing, and me, poor lowly maid,
Most goddess-like prank'd up: but that our feasts 10
In every mess have folly, and the feeders
Digest it with a custom, I should blush
To see you so attired; swoon, I think,
To show myself a glass.
 *Flo.*     I bless the time
When my good falcon made her flight across
Thy father's ground.
 *Per.*    Now Jove afford you cause!
To me the difference forges dread; your greatness
Hath not been us'd to fear.  Even now I tremble
To think your father, by some accident,
Should pass this way as you did: O the Fates! 20
How would he look, to see his work, so noble,
Vilely bound up?  What would he say?  Or how
Should I, in these my borrow'd flaunts, behold
The sternness of his presence?
 *Flo.*     Apprehend
Nothing but jollity.  The gods themselves,
Humbling their deities to love, have taken
The shapes of beasts upon them: Jupiter
Became a bull, and bellow'd; the green Neptune
A ram, and bleated; and the fire-rob'd god,
Golden Apollo, a poor humble swain, 30
As I seem now.  Their transformations
Were never for a piece of beauty rarer,
Nor in a way so chaste, since my desires
Run not before mine honour, nor my lusts
Burn hotter than my faith.
 *Per.*    O but, sir,

Your resolution cannot hold, when 't is
Oppos'd, as it must be, by the power of the king:
One of these two must be necessities,
Which then will speak, that you must change this
        purpose,
Or I my life.

   *Flo.*       Thou dearest Perdita,      40
With these forc'd thoughts, I prithee, darken not
The mirth o' the feast.   Or I 'll be thine, my fair,
Or not my father's; for I cannot be
Mine own, nor any thing to any, if
I be not thine: to this I am most constant,
Though destiny say no.   Be merry, gentle;
Strangle such thoughts as these with any thing
That you behold the while.   Your guests are coming:
Lift up your countenance, as it were the day
Of celebration of that nuptial which      50
We two have sworn shall come.

   *Per.*            O Lady Fortune,
Stand you auspicious!

   *Flo.*          See, your guests approach:
Address yourself to entertain them sprightly,
And let 's be red with mirth.

*Enter* Shepherd, *with* POLIXENES *and* CAMILLO *disguised;*
    Clown, MOPSA, DORCAS, *and other* Shepherds *and*
    Shepherdesses.

   *Shep.*   Fie, daughter! when my old wife liv'd, upon
This day she was both pantler, butler, cook,
Both dame and servant; welcom'd all, serv'd all;
Would sing her song and dance her turn; now here,
At upper end o' the table, now i' the middle;
On his shoulder, and his; her face o' fire      60
With labour, and the thing she took to quench it,
She would to each one sip.   You are retir'd,

As if you were a feasted one, and not
The hostess of the meeting: pray you, bid
These unknown friends to 's welcome; for it is
A way to make us better friends, more known.
Come, quench your blushes and present yourself
That which you are, mistress o' the feast: come on,
And bid us welcome to your sheep-shearing,
As your good flock shall prosper.

 *Per.* [*To Polixenes*]   Sir, welcome: 70
It is my father's will I should take on me
The hostess-ship o' the day. [*To Camillo*] You're
  welcome, sir.
Give me those flowers there, Dorcas. Reverend sirs,
For you there 's rosemary and rue; these keep
Seeming and savour all the winter long:
Grace and remembrance be to you both,
And welcome to our shearing!

 *Pol.*       Shepherdess,
A fair one are you, well you fit our ages
With flowers of winter.

 *Per.*     Sir, the year growing ancient,
Not yet on summer's death, nor on the birth 80
Of trembling winter, the fairest flowers o' the season
Are our carnations and streak'd gillyvors,
Which some call nature's bastards: of that kind
Our rustic garden 's barren; and I care not
To get slips of them.

 *Pol.*    Wherefore, gentle maiden,
Do you neglect them?

 *Per.*    For I have heard it said
There is an art which in their piedness shares
With great creating nature.

 *Pol.*     Say there be;
Yet nature is made better by no mean,
But nature makes that mean: so, o'er that art 90

Which you say adds to nature, is an art
That nature makes.   You see, sweet maid, we marry
A gentler scion to the wildest stock,
And make conceive a bark of baser kind
By bud of nobler race: this is an art
Which does mend nature, change it rather, but
The art itself is nature.
   *Per.*          So it is.
   *Pol.* Then make your garden rich in gillyvors,
And do not call them bastards.
   *Per.*           I 'll not put
The dibble in earth to set one slip of them;     100
No more than were I painted I would wish
This youth should say 't were well, and only therefore
Desire to breed by me.   Here 's flowers for you;
Hot lavender, mints, savory, marjoram;
The marigold, that goes to bed wi' the sun
And with him rises weeping: these are flowers
Of middle summer, and I think they are given
To men of middle age.   You 're very welcome.
   *Cam.* I should leave grazing, were I of your flock,
And only live by gazing.
   *Per.*          Out, alas!     110
You 'd be so lean, that blasts of January
Would blow you through and through.   Now my fair'st
    friend,
I would I had some flowers o' the spring that might
Become your time of day; O Proserpina,     116
For the flowers now, that frighted thou lett'st fall
From Dis's wagon! daffodils,
That come before the swallow dares, and take
The winds of March with beauty; violets dim,    120
But sweeter than the lids of Juno's eyes
Or Cytherea's breath; pale primroses,
That die unmarried, ere they can behold

Bright Phœbus in his strength, a malady
Most incident to maids; bold oxlips and
The crown imperial; lilies of all kinds,
The flower-de-luce being one!   O, these I lack,
To make you garlands of; and my sweet friend,
To strew him o'er and o'er!
   *Flo.*                What, like a corse?
   *Per.*   No, like a bank for love to lie and play on;   130
Not like a corse; or if, not to be buried,
But quick, and in mine arms.   Come, take your flowers:
Methinks I play as I have seen them do
In Whitsun pastorals: sure, this robe of mine
Does change my disposition.
   *Flo.*                What you do
Still betters what is done.   When you speak, sweet,
I'd have you do it ever: when you sing,
I'd have you buy and sell so, so give alms,
Pray so; and, for the ordering your affairs,
To sing them too: when you do dance, I wish you   140
A wave o' the sea, that you might ever do
Nothing but that; move still, still so,
And own no other function: each your doing,
So singular in each particular,
Crowns what you are doing in the present deeds,
That all your acts are queens.
   *Per.*              O Doricles,
Your praises are too large: but that your youth,
And the true blood which peeps fairly through 't,
Do plainly give you out an unstain'd shepherd,
With wisdom I might fear, my Doricles,   150
You woo'd me the false way.
   *Flo.*            I think you have
As little skill to fear as I have purpose
To put you to 't.   But, come; our dance, I pray:
Your hand, my Perdita: so turtles pair,

That never mean to part.
    *Per.*                 I 'll swear for 'em.
    *Pol.* This is the prettiest low-born lass that ever
Ran on the green-sward: nothing she does or seems
But smacks of something greater than herself,
Too noble for this place.
    *Cam.*            He tells her something
That makes her blood look out: good sooth, she is  160
The queen of curds and cream.
    *Clo.*             Come on, strike up!
    *Dor.* Mopsa must be your mistress: marry, garlic,
To mend her kissing with!
    *Mop.*          Now, in good time!
    *Clo.* Not a word, a word; we stand upon our manners.
Come, strike up!
             [*Music.  Here a dance of Shepherds and
                 Shepherdesses.*
    *Pol.* Pray, good shepherd, what fair swain is this
Which dances with your daughter?
    *Shep.* They call him Doricles; and boasts himself
To have a worthy feeding: but I have it
Upon his own report and I believe it;          170
He looks like sooth.  He says he loves my daughter:
I think so too; for never gaz'd the moon
Upon the water, as he 'll stand, and read
As 't were my daughter's eyes: and, to be plain,
I think there is not half a kiss to choose
Who loves another best.
    *Pol.*          She dances featly.
    *Shep.* So she does any thing; though I report it,
That should be silent: if young Doricles
Do light upon her, she shall bring him that
Which he not dreams of.                 180

*Enter* Servant

*Serv.* O master, if you did but hear the pedlar at the
door, you would never dance again after a tabor and
pipe; no, the bagpipe could not move you: he sings
several tunes faster than you'll tell money; he utters
them as he had eaten ballads and all men's ears grew
to his tunes.

*Clo.* He could never come better; he shall come in.
I love a ballad but even too well, if it be doleful matter
merrily set down, or a very pleasant thing indeed and
sung lamentably.                                    190

*Serv.* He hath songs for man or woman, of all sizes;
no milliner can so fit his customers with gloves: he has
the prettiest love-songs for maids; so without bawdry,
which is strange; with such delicate burdens of dildos
and fadings, "jump her and thump her."

*Pol.* This is a brave fellow.

*Clo.* Believe me, thou talkest of an admirable conceited fellow.   Has he any unbraided wares?      198

*Serv.* He hath ribands of all the colours i' the rain-
bow; points more than all the lawyers in Bohemia can
learnedly handle, though they come to him by the gross;
inkles, caddises, cambrics, lawns: why, he sings 'em
over, as they were gods or goddesses; you would think
a smock were a she-angel, he so chants to the sleeve-
hand and the work about the square on 't.

*Clo.* Prithee, bring him in; and let him approach
singing.

*Per.* Forewarn him that he use no scurrilous words
in 's tunes.                                    [*Exit Servant.*

*Clo.* You have of these pedlars, that have more in
in them than you'd think, sister.                 211

*Per.* Ay, good brother, or go about to think.

*Enter* AUTOLYCUS, *singing*

Lawn as white as driven snow;
Cyprus black as e'er was crow;
Gloves as sweet as damask roses;
Masks for faces and for noses;
Bugle bracelet, necklace amber,
Perfume for a lady's chamber;
Golden quoifs and stomachers,
For my lads to give their dears;                    220
Pins and poking-sticks of steel,
What maids lack from head to heel
Come buy of me, come; come buy, come buy;
Buy, lads, or else your lasses cry:
Come buy.

*Clo.* If I were not in love with Mopsa, thou shouldst take no money of me; but being enthrall'd as I am, it will also be the bondage of certain ribands and gloves.

*Mop.* I was promised them against the feast; but they come not too late now.                    230

*Dor.* He hath promis'd you more than that, or there be liars.

*Mop.* He hath paid you all he promis'd you: may be, he has paid you more, which will shame you to give him again.

*Clo.* Is there no manners left among maids? will they wear their plackets where they should bear their faces? Is there not milking-time, when you are going to bed, or kiln-hole, to whistle-off these secrets, but you must be tittle-tattling before all our guests? 'Tis well they are whispering: clamour your tongues, and not a word more.                    242

*Mop.* I have done. Come, you promis'd me a tawdry-lace and a pair of sweet gloves.

*Clo.* Have I not told thee how I was cozen'd by the way, and lost all my money?

*Aut.* And, indeed, sir, there are cozeners abroad; therefore it behoves men to be wary.

*Clo.* Fear not thou, man, thou shalt lose nothing here.

*Aut.* I hope so, sir; for I have about me many parcels of charge.                                                                251

*Clo.* What hast here? ballads?

*Mop.* Pray now, buy some: I love a ballad in print a life, for then we are sure they are true.

*Aut.* Here's one to a very doleful tune, how a usurer's wife was brought to bed of twenty money-bags at a burthen, and how she long'd to eat adders' heads and toads carbonadoed.

*Mop.* Is it true, think you?

*Aut.* Very true, and but a month old.                          260

*Dor.* Bless me from marrying a usurer!

*Aut.* Here's the midwife's name to 't, one Mrs. Taleporter, and five or six honest wives that were present. Why should I carry lies abroad?

*Mop.* Pray you now, buy it.

*Clo.* Come on, lay it by: and let's first see moe ballads; we'll buy the other things anon.

*Aut.* Here's another ballad of a fish, that appeared upon the coast on Wednesday the fourscore of April, forty thousand fathom above water, and sung this ballad against the hard hearts of maids: it was thought she was a woman, and was turn'd into a cold fish for she would not exchange flesh with one that lov'd her: the ballad is very pitiful, and as true.                          274

*Dor.* Is it true too, think you?

*Aut.* Five justices' hands at it, and witnesses more than my pack will hold.

*Clo.* Lay it by too: another.

*Aut.* This is a merry ballad, but a very pretty one.

*Mop.* Let's have some merry ones.                          280

*Aut.* Why, this is a passing merry one, and goes to

the tune of "Two maids wooing a man:" there's scarce
a maid westward but she sings it; 'tis in request, I can
tell you.

*Mop.* We can both sing it: if thou 'lt bear a part, thou
shalt hear; 'tis in three parts.

*Dor.* We had the tune on 't a month ago.

*Aut.* I can bear my part; you must know 'tis my
occupation: have at it with you!

### Song

    *Aut.* Get you hence, for I must go         290
Where it fits not you to know.
   *Dor.* Whither?  *Mop.* O whither?  *Dor.* Whither?
*Mop.* It becomes thy oath full well,
Thou to me thy secrets tell:
   *Dor.* Me too, let me go thither.

*Mop.* Or thou goest to the grange or mill:
*Dor.* If to either, thou dost ill.
   *Aut.* Neither.  *Dor.* What neither?  *Aut.* Neither.
*Dor.* Thou hast sworn my love to be;
*Mop.* Thou hast sworn it more to me:     300
   Then, whither goest? say, whither?

*Clo.* We 'll have this song out anon by ourselves: my
father and the gentlemen are in sad talk, and we 'll not
trouble them.  Come, bring away thy pack after me.
Wenches, I 'll buy for you both.  Pedlar, let's have the
first choice.  Follow me, girls.

                [*Exit with Dorcas and Mopsa.*
*Aut.* And you shall pay well for 'em.

                [*Follows singing.*
       Will you buy any tape,
       Or lace for your cape,
    My dainty duck, my dear-a?     310
       Any silk, any thread,
       Any toys for your head,
   Of the new'st and fin'st, fin'st wear-a?

> Come to the pedlar;
> Money 's a meddler,
> That doth utter all men's ware-a.

[*Exit.*

*Re-enter* Servant

*Serv.* Master, there is three carters, three shepherds, three neat-herds, three swine-herds, that have made themselves all men of hair, they call themselves Saltiers, and they have a dance which the wenches say is a gallimaufry of gambols, because they are not in 't; but they themselves are o' the mind, if it be not too rough for some that know little but bowling, it will please plentifully.                                    324

*Shep.* Away! we 'll none on 't: here has been too much homely foolery already.  I know, sir, we weary you.

*Pol.* You weary those that refresh us: pray, let 's see these four threes of herdsmen.                         329

*Serv.* One three of them, by their own report, sir, hath danc'd before the king; and not the worst of the three but jumps twelve foot and a half by the squier.

*Shep.* Leave your prating: since these good men are pleas'd, let them come in; but quickly now.

*Serv.* Why, they stay at door, sir.              [*Exit.*

*Here a dance of twelve Satyrs*

*Pol.* O father, you 'll know more of that hereafter.
[*To Camillo.*] Is it not too far gone?   'T is time to part
    them.
He 's simple and tells much.   How now, fair shepherd!
Your heart is full of something that does take      339
Your mind from feasting.   Sooth, when I was young,
And handed love as you do, I was wont
To load my she with knacks: I would have ransack'd
The pedlar's silken treasury, and have pour'd it

To her acceptance; you have let him go
And nothing marted with him.   If your lass
Interpretation should abuse, and call this
Your lack of love or bounty, you were straited
For a reply, at least if you make a care
Of happy holding her.
  *Flo.*      Old sir, I know
She prizes not such trifles as these are:   350
The gifts she looks from me are pack'd and lock'd
Up in my heart; which I have given already,
But not deliver'd.   O, hear me breathe my life
Before this ancient sir, who, it should seem,
Hath sometime lov'd!   I take thy hand, this hand,
As soft as dove's down and as white as it,
Or Ethiopian's tooth, or the fann'd snow that's bolted
By the northern blasts twice o'er.
  *Pol.*      What follows this.
How prettily the young swain seems to wash
The hand was fair before!   I have put you out:  360
But to your protestation; let me hear
What you profess.
  *Flo.*    Do, and be witness to't.
  *Pol.* And this my neighbour too?
  *Flo.*      And he, and more
Than he, and men, the earth, the heavens, and all:
That, were I crown'd the most imperial monarch,
Thereof most worthy, were I the fairest youth
That ever made eye swerve, had force and knowledge
More than was ever man's, I would not prize them
Without her love; for her employ them all;
Commend them and condemn them to her service  370
Or to their own perdition.
  *Pol.*     Fairly offer'd.
  *Cam.* This shows a sound affection.
  *Shep.*       But my daughter,

Say you the like to him?

*Per.*                    I cannot speak
So well, nothing so well; no, nor mean better:
By the pattern of mine own thoughts I cut out
The purity of his.

   *Shep.*          Take hands, a bargain!
And, friends unknown, you shall bear witness to 't:
I give my daughter to him, and will make
Her portion equal his.

   *Flo.*                    O, that must be
I' the virtue of your daughter; one being dead,          380
I shall have more than you can dream of yet;
Enough then for your wonder.   But, come on,
Contract us 'fore these witnesses.

   *Shep.*                      Come, your hand;
And, daughter, yours.

   *Pol.*                  Soft, swain, awhile, beseech you;
Have you a father?

   *Flo.*            I have: but what of him?

   *Pol.* Knows he of this?

   *Flo.*                  He neither does nor shall.

   *Pol.* Methinks a father
Is, at the nuptial of his son, a guest
That best becomes the table.   Pray you, once more,
Is not your father grown incapable          390
Of reasonable affairs? is he not stupid
With age and altering rheums? can he speak? hear?
Know man from man? dispute his own estate?
Lies he not bed-rid? and again does nothing
But what he did being childish?

   *Flo.*                  No, good sir;
He has his health, and ampler strength indeed
Than most have of his age.

   *Pol.*                By my white beard,
You offer him, if this be so, a wrong

Something unfilial: reason my son
Should choose himself a wife, but as good reason          400
The father, all whose joy is nothing else
But fair posterity, should hold some counsel
In such a business.

    *Flo.*             I yield all this;
But, for some other reasons, my grave sir,
Which 't is not fit you know, I not acquaint
My father of this business.

    *Pol.*             Let him know 't.

    *Flo.* He shall not.

    *Pol.*             Prithee, let him.

    *Flo.*                 No, he must not.

    *Shep.* Let him, my son: he shall not need to grieve
At knowing of thy choice.

    *Flo.*          Come, come, he must not.—
Mark our contráct.

    *Pol.*        Mark your divorce, young sir,          410
                      *[Throws off his disguise.*
Whom son I dare not call; thou art too base
To be acknowledged: thou a sceptre's heir,
That thus affects a sheep-hook! Thou old traitor,
I am sorry that by hanging thee I can but
Shorten thy life one week.—And thou, fresh piece
Of excellent witchcraft, who of force must know
The royal fool thou cop'st with,—

    *Shep.*             O my heart!

    *Pol.* I 'll have thy beauty scratch'd with briers, and
        made
More homely than thy state. For thee, fond boy,
If I may ever know thou dost but sigh          420
That thou no more shalt see this knack as never
I mean thou shalt, we 'll bar thee from succession;
Not hold thee of our blood, no, not our kin,
Farre than Deucalion off: mark thou my words:

Follow us to the court.   Thou churl, for this time,
Though full of our displeasure, yet we free thee
From the dead blow of it.   And you, enchantment,—
Worthy enough a herdsman,—yea, him too
That makes himself, but for our honour therein,
Unworthy thee,—if ever henceforth thou        430
These rural latches to his entrance open,
Or hoop his body more with thy embraces,
I will devise a death as cruel for thee
As thou art tender to 't.                     [*Exit.*

   *Per.*               Even here undone!
I was not much afeard; for once or twice
I was about to speak and tell him plainly,
The selfsame sun that shines upon his court
Hides not his visage from our cottage, but
Looks on alike.   [*To Florizel*] Will 't please you, sir,
    be gone?
I told you what would come of this: beseech you,   440
Of your own state take care: this dream of mine,—
Being now awake, I 'll queen it no inch farther,
But milk my ewes and weep.

   *Cam.*               What, how now, father!
Speak ere thou diest.

   *Shep.*               I cannot speak, nor think,
Nor dare to know that which I know.   [*To Florizel*] O
    sir,
You have undone a man of fourscore three,
That thought to fill his grave in quiet; yea,
To die upon the bed my father died,
To lie close by his honest bones: but now
Some hangman must put on my shroud and lay me  450
Where no priest shovels in dust.   [*To Perdita*] O
    cursed wretch,
That knew'st this was the prince, and wouldst adventure
To mingle faith with him!   Undone! undone!

If I might die within this hour, I have liv'd
To die when I desire.                              [*Exit.*

   *Flo.*                    Why look you so upon me?
I am but sorry, not afeard, delay'd,
But nothing alter'd: what I was. I am;
More straining on for plucking back, not following
My leash unwillingly.

   *Cam.*                    Gracious my lord,
You know your father's temper: at this time        460
He will allow no speech, which I do guess
You do not purpose to him; and as hardly
Will he endure your sight as yet, I fear:
Then, till the fury of his highness settle,
Come not before him.

   *Flo.*                    I not purpose it.
I think, Camillo?

   *Cam.*          Even he, my lord.

   *Per.* How often have I told you 't would be thus!
How often said my dignity would last
But till 't were known!

   *Flo.*                    It cannot fail but by
The violation of my faith; and then                470
Let nature crush the sides o' the earth together
And mar the seeds within! Lift up thy looks:
From my succession wipe me, father, I
Am heir to my affection.

   *Cam.*                    Be advis'd.

   *Flo.* I am, and by my fancy: if my reason
Will thereto be obedient, I have reason;
If not, my senses, better pleas'd with madness,
Do bid it welcome.

   *Cam.*          This is desperate, sir.

   *Flo.* So call it: but it does fulfil my vow;
I needs must think it honesty. Camillo,              480
Not for Bohemia, nor the pomp that may

Be thereat glean'd; for all the sun sees, or
The close earth wombs, or the profound seas hides
In unknown fathoms, will I break my oath
To this my fair belov'd; therefore, I pray you,
As you have ever been my father's honour'd friend,
When he shall miss me,—as, in faith, I mean not
To see him any more,—cast your good counsels
Upon his passion: let myself and fortune
Tug for the time to come. This you may know,    490
And so deliver, I am put to sea
With her who here I cannot hold on shore;
And most opportune to her need I have
A vessel rides fast by, but not prepar'd
For this design. What course I mean to hold
Shall nothing benefit your knowledge, nor
Concern me the reporting.

    *Cam.*               O my lord,
I would your spirit were easier for advice,
Or stronger for your need!

    *Flo.*           Hark, Perdita. [*Draws her aside.*
[*To Camillo*] I'll hear you by and by.

    *Cam.*               He's irremovable,
Resolv'd for flight. Now were I happy, if    501
His going I could frame to serve my turn,
Save him from danger, do him love and honour,
Purchase the sight again of dear Sicilia,
And that unhappy king my master, whom
I so much thirst to see.

    *Flo.*           Now, good Camillo;
I am so fraught with curious business that
I leave out ceremony.

    *Cam.*         Sir, I think
You have heard of my poor services, i' the love
That I have borne your father?

    *Flo.*           Very nobly    510
4                          (D 656)

Have you deserv'd: it is my father's music
To speak your deeds, not little of his care
To have them recompens'd as thought on.

 *Cam.*          Well, my lord,
If you may please to think I love the king,
And through him what is nearest to him, which is
Your gracious self, embrace but my direction,
If your more ponderous and settled project
May suffer alteration, on mine honour
I'll point you where you shall have such receiving   520
As shall become your highness; where you may
Enjoy your mistress, from the whom, I see,
There's no disjunction to be made, but by—
As heavens forefend!—your ruin; marry her,
And, with my best endeavours in your absence,
Your discontenting father strive to qualify
And bring him up to liking.

 *Flo.*        How, Camillo,
May this, almost a miracle, be done?
That I may call thee something more than man
And after that trust to thee.

 *Cam.*        Have you thought on   530
A place whereto you'll go?

 *Flo.*        Not any yet:
But as the unthought-on accident is guilty
To what we wildly do, so we profess
Ourselves to be the slaves of chance, and flies
Of every wind that blows.

 *Cam.*       Then list to me:
This follows, if you will not change your purpose,
But undergo this flight, make for Sicilia,
And there present yourself and your fair princess,
For so I see she must be, 'fore Leontes:
She shall be habited as it becomes      540
The partner of your bed. Methinks I see

Leontes opening his free arms and weeping
His welcomes forth; asks thee the son forgiveness,
As 't were i' the father's person; kisses the hands
Of your fresh princess; o'er and o'er divides him
'Twixt his unkindness and his kindness; the one
He chides to hell and bids the other grow
Faster than thought or time.

    *Flo.*                    Worthy Camillo,
What colour for my visitation shall I
Hold up before him?

    *Cam.*           Sent by the king your father   550
To greet him and to give him comforts.   Sir,
The manner of your bearing towards him, with
What you as from your father shall deliver,
Things known betwixt us three, I 'll write you down:
The which shall point you forth at every sitting
What you must say; that he shall not perceive
But that you have your father's bosom there,
And speak his very heart.

    *Flo.*               I am bound to you:
There is some sap in this.

    *Cam.*           A course more promising
Than a wild dedication of yourselves   560
To unpath'd waters, undream'd shores, most certain
To miseries enough: no hope to help you,
But, as you shake off one to take another:
Nothing so certain as your anchors, who
Do their best office, if they can but stay you
Where you 'll be loth to be: besides you know
Prosperity 's the very bond of love,
Whose fresh complexion and whose heart together
Affliction alters.

    *Per.*         One of these is true:
I think affliction may subdue the cheek,   570
But not take in the mind.

*Cam.*                    Yea, say you so?
There shall not at your father's house these seven years
Be born another such.
    *Flo.*                    My good Camillo,
She is as forward of her breeding as
She is i' the rear o' her birth.
    *Cam.*                    I cannot say 't is pity
She lacks instructions, for she seems a mistress
To most that teach.
    *Per.*               Your pardon, sir; for this
I 'll blush you thanks.
    *Flo.*                    My prettiest Perdita!
But O the thorns we stand upon! Camillo,
Preserver of my father, now of me,                    580
The medicine of our house, how shall we do?
We are not furnish'd like Bohemia's son,
Nor shall appear in Sicilia.
    *Cam.*                    My lord,
Fear none of this: I think you know my fortunes
Do all lie there: it shall be so my care
To have you royally appointed as if
The scene you play were mine. For instance, sir,     587
That you may know you shall not want,—one word.
                       *[They talk aside.*

### *Re-enter* AUTOLYCUS

    *Aut.* Ha, ha! what a fool Honesty is! and Trust, his
sworn brother, a very simple gentleman! I have sold
all my trumpery; not a counterfeit stone, not a riband,
glass, pomander, brooch, table-book, ballad, knife, tape,
glove, shoe-tie, bracelet, horn-ring, to keep my pack
from fasting: they throng who should buy first, as if
my trinkets had been hallowed and brought a bene-
diction to the buyer: by which means I saw whose
purse was best in picture; and what I saw, to my good

use I remember'd.  My clown, who wants but something to be a reasonable man, grew so in love with the wenches' song, that he would not stir his pettitoes till he had both tune and words; which so drew the rest of the herd to me, that all their other senses stuck in ears; you might have pinch'd a placket, it was senseless; I would have fil'd keys off that hung in chains; no hearing, no feeling, but my sir's song, and admiring the nothing of it.  So that, in this time of lethargy, I pick'd and cut most of their festival purses; and had not the old man come in with a whoo-bub against his daughter and the king's son, and scar'd my choughs from the chaff, I had not left a purse alive in the whole army.     [*Camillo, Florizel, and Perdita come forward.*

*Cam.*  Nay, but my letters, by this means being there
So soon as you arrive, shall clear that doubt.          613

*Flo.*  And those that you 'll procure from King
     Leontes—

*Cam.*  Shall satisfy your father.

*Per.*                              Happy be you!
All that you speak shows fair.

*Cam.*  [*Sees Autolycus*] Who have we here?
We 'll make an instrument of this; omit
Nothing may give us aid.

*Aut.*  If they have overheard me now, why, hanging.

*Cam.*  How now, good fellow! why shak'st thou so?
Fear not, man; here 's no harm intended to thee.     621

*Aut.*  I am a poor fellow, sir.

*Cam.*  Why, be so still; here 's nobody will steal that from thee: yet, for the outside of thy poverty we must make an exchange; therefore discase thee instantly,— thou must think there 's a necessity in 't,—and change garments with this gentleman: though the pennyworth on his side be the worst, yet hold thee, there 's some boot.

*Aut.* I am a poor fellow, sir.   [*Aside*] I know ye well
enough.                                                               631

*Cam.* Nay, prithee, dispatch: the gentleman is half
flay'd already.

*Aut.* Are you in earnest, sir?   [*Aside*] I smell the
trick on 't.

*Flo.* Dispatch, I prithee.

*Aut.* Indeed, I have had earnest; but I cannot with
conscience take it.

*Cam.* Unbuckle, unbuckle.—

                    [*Florizel and Autolycus change garments.*
Fortunate mistress,—let my prophecy                 640
Come home to ye!—you must retire yourself
Into some covert: take your sweetheart's hat
And pluck it o'er your brows, muffle your face,
Dismantle you, and, as you can, disliken
The truth of your own seeming; that you may—
For I do fear eyes over—to shipboard
Get undescried.

*Per.*                I see the play so lies
That I must bear a part.

*Cam.*                      No remedy.
Have you done there?

*Flo.*                      Should I now meet my father,
He would not call me son.

*Cam.*                            Nay, you shall have no hat.
                              [*Giving it to Perdita.*
Come, lady, come.   Farewell, my friend.

*Aut.*                                        Adieu, sir.

*Flo.* O Perdita, what have we twain forgot!        652
Pray you, a word.

*Cam.* [*Aside*] What I do next, shall be to tell the king
Of this escape and whither they are bound;
Wherein, my hope is, I shall so prevail
To force him after: in whose company

I shall review Sicilia, for whose sight
I have a woman's longing.
    *Flo.*                Fortune speed us!
Thus we set on, Camillo, to the sea-side.      660
    *Cam.* The swifter speed the better.

          [*Exeunt Florizel, Perdita, and Camillo.*

    *Aut.* I understand the business, I hear it: to have an
open ear, a quick eye, and a nimble hand, is necessary
for a cut-purse; a good nose is requisite also, to smell
out work for the other senses. I see this is the time
that the unjust man doth thrive. What an exchange
had this been without boot! What a boot is here with
this exchange! Sure the gods do this year connive at
us, and we may do any thing extempore. The prince
himself is about a piece of iniquity, stealing away from
his father with his clog at his heels: if I thought it
were a piece of honesty to acquaint the king withal,
I would not do 't: I hold it the more knavery to conceal
it; and therein am I constant to my profession.    674

        *Re-enter* Clown *and* Shepherd

Aside, aside; here is more matter for a hot brain: every
lane's end, every shop, church, session, hanging, yields
a careful man work.
    *Clo.* See, see; what a man you are now! There is
no other way but to tell the king she's a changeling
and none of your flesh and blood.      680
    *Shep.* Nay, but hear me.
    *Clo.* Nay, but hear me.
    *Shep.* Go to, then.
    *Clo.* She being none of your flesh and blood, your
flesh and blood has not offended the king; and so your
flesh and blood is not to be punish'd by him. Show
those things you found about her, those secret things,

all but what she has with her: this being done, let the
law go whistle: I warrant you.                    689

*Shep.* I will tell the king all, every word, yea, and
his son's pranks too; who, I may say, is no honest man,
neither to his father nor to me, to go about to make me
the king's brother-in-law.

*Clo.* Indeed, brother-in-law was the furthest off you
could have been to him, and then your blood had been
the dearer by I know how much an ounce.

*Aut.* [*Aside*] Very wisely, puppies!

*Shep.* Well, let us to the king: there is that in this
fardel will make him scratch his beard.          699

*Aut.* [*Aside*] I know not what impediment the complaint may be to the flight of my master.

*Clo.* Pray heartily he be at palace.

*Aut.* [*Aside*] Though I am not naturally honest, I am
so sometimes by chance: let me pocket up my pedler's
excrement.    [*Takes off his false beard.*]    How now,
rustics! whither are you bound?

*Shep.* To the palace, an it like your worship.

*Aut.* Your affairs there, what, with whom, the condition of that fardel, the place of your dwelling, your
names, your ages, of what having, breeding, and any
thing that is fitting to be known, discover.      711

*Clo.* We are but plain fellows, sir.

*Aut.* A lie; you are rough and hairy.  Let me have
no lying: it becomes none but tradesmen, and they often
give us soldiers the lie: but we pay them for it with
stamped coin, not stabbing steel; therefore they do not
give us the lie.

*Clo.* Your worship had like to have given us one, if
you had not taken yourself with the manner.

*Shep.* Are you a courtier, an 't like you, sir?     720

*Aut.* Whether it like me or no, I am a courtier.  Seest
thou not the air of the court in these enfoldings? hath

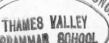

not my gait in it the measure of the court? receive not
thy nose court-odour from me? reflect I not on thy
baseness court-contempt?   Think'st thou, for that I
insinuate, or toaze from thee thy business, I am therefore no courtier?   I am courtier cap-a-pe; and one that
will either push on or pluck back thy business there:
whereupon I command thee to open thy affair.

*Shep.* My business, sir, is to the king.          730

*Aut.* What advocate hast thou to him?

*Shep.* I know not, an 't like you.

*Clo.* [*Aside to Shepherd*] Advocate 's the court word
for a pheasant: say you have none.

*Shep.* None, sir; I have no pheasant, cock nor hen.

*Aut.* How blessed are we that are not simple men!
Yet nature might have made me as these are,
Therefore I will not disdain.

*Clo.* [*Aside to Shepherd*] This cannot be but a great
courtier.          740

*Shep.* [*Aside to Clown*] His garments are rich, but he
wears them not handsomely.

*Clo.* [*Aside to Shepherd*] He seems to be the more
noble in being fantastical: a great man, I 'll warrant; I
know by the picking on 's teeth.

*Aut.* The fardel there? what 's i' the fardel?   Wherefore that box?

*Shep.* Sir, there lies such secrets in this fardel and
box, which none must know but the king; and which he
shall know within this hour, if I may come to the speech
of him.          751

*Aut.* Age, thou hast lost thy labour.

*Shep.* Why, sir?

*Aut.* The king is not at the palace; he is gone aboard
a new ship to purge melancholy and air himself: for, if
thou beest capable of things serious, thou must know
the king is full of grief.

4•          (D 656)

*Shep.* So 't is said, sir; about his son, that should
have married a shepherd's daughter.

*Aut.* If that shepherd be not in hand-fast, let him fly:
the curses he shall have, the tortures he shall feel, will
break the back of man, the heart of monster.      762

*Clo.* Think you so, sir?

*Aut.* Not he alone shall suffer what wit can make
heavy and vengeance bitter; but those that are germane
to him, though remov'd fifty times, shall all come under
the hangman: which though it be great pity, yet it is
necessary.   An old sheep-whistling rogue, a ram-tender,
to offer to have his daughter come into grace!   Some
say he shall be ston'd; but that death is too soft for him,
say I: draw our throne into a sheep-cote! all deaths are
too few, the sharpest too easy.      772

*Clo.* Has the old man e'er a son, sir, do you hear,
an 't like you, sir?

*Aut.* He has a son, who shall be flay'd alive; then
'nointed over with honey, set on the head of a wasps'
nest; then stand till he be three-quarters and a dram
dead; then recover'd again with aqua-vitæ or some
other hot infusion; then, raw as he is, and in the hottest
day prognostication proclaims, shall he be set against a
brick-wall, the sun looking with a southward eye upon
him, where he is to behold him with flies blown to death.
But what talk we of these traitorly rascals, whose
miseries are to be smil'd at, their offences being so
capital?   Tell me, for you seem to be honest plain men,
what you have to the king: being something gently
consider'd, I 'll bring you where he is aboard, tender
your persons to his presence, whisper him in your
behalfs; and if it be in man besides the king to effect
your suits, here is man shall do it.      790

*Clo.* [*Aside to Shepherd*] He seems to be of great
authority: close with him, give him gold: and though

authority be a stubborn bear, yet he is oft led by the nose with gold: show the inside of your purse to the outside of his hand, and no more ado. Remember, "ston'd," and "flay'd alive."

*Shep.* An 't please you, sir, to undertake the business for us, here is that gold I have: I 'll make it as much more and leave this young man in pawn till I bring it you. 800

*Aut.* After I have done what I promised?

*Shep.* Ay, sir.

*Aut.* Well, give me the moiety. Are you a party in this business?

*Clo.* In some sort, sir: but though my case be a pitiful one, I hope I shall not be flay'd out of it.

*Aut.* O, that 's the case of the shepherd's son: hang him, he 'll be made an example. 808

*Clo.* [*To Shepherd*] Comfort, good comfort! We must to the king and show our strange sights: he must know 't is none of your daughter nor my sister; we are gone else. Sir, I will give you as much as this old man does when the business is performed; and remain, as he says, your pawn till it be brought you.

*Aut.* I will trust you. Walk before towards the sea-side; go on the right hand: I will but look upon the hedge and follow you.

*Clo.* We are blest in this man, as I may say, even blest. 819

*Shep.* Let 's before, as he bids us: he was provided to do us good. [*Exeunt Shepherd and Clown.*

*Aut.* If I had a mind to be honest, I see Fortune would not suffer me: she drops booties in my mouth. I am courted now with a double occasion, gold and a means to do the prince my master good; which who knows how that may turn back to my advancement? I will bring these two moles, these blind ones, aboard

him: if he think it fit to shore them again and that the
complaint they have to the king concerns him nothing,
let him call me rogue for being so far officious; for I
am proof against that title, and what shame else belongs
to 't.   To him will I present them: there may be matter
in it.                                                    [*Exit.*

---

## ACT V

### Scene I.   *A room in Leontes' palace*

*Enter* Leontes, Cleomenes, Dion, Paulina,
*and* Servants

   *Cleo.* Sir, you have done enough, and have perform'd
A saint-like sorrow: no fault could you make,
Which you have not redeem'd; indeed, paid down
More penitence than done trespass: at the last,
Do as the heavens have done, forget your evil;
With them, forgive yourself.
   *Leon.*                      Whilst I remember
Her and her virtues, I cannot forget
My blemishes in them; and so still think of
The wrong I did myself: which was so much,
That heirless it hath made my kingdom and          10
Destroy'd the sweet'st companion that e'er man
Bred his hopes out of.
   *Paul.*               True, too true, my lord:
If, one by one, you wedded all the world,
Or from the all that are took something good,
To make a perfect woman, she you kill'd
Would be unparallel'd.
   *Leon.*             I think so.   Kill'd!
She I kill'd! I did so: but thou strikest me

Sorely, to say I did; it is as bitter
Upon thy tongue as in my thought: now, good now,
Say so but seldom.
   *Cleo.*          Not at all, good lady:   20
You might have spoken a thousand things that would
Have done the time more benefit and grac'd
Your kindness better.
   *Paul.*        You are one of those
Would have him wed again.
   *Dion.*          If you would not so,
You pity not the state, nor the remembrance
Of his most sovereign name; consider little
What dangers, by his highness' fail of issue,
May drop upon his kingdom and devour
Incertain lookers on.   What were more holy
Than to rejoice the former queen is well?   30
What holier than, for royalty's repair,
For present comfort, and for future good,
To bless the bed of majesty again
With a sweet fellow to 't?
   *Paul.*        There is none worthy,
Respecting her that 's gone.   Besides, the gods
Will have fulfill'd their secret purposes;
For has not the divine Apollo said,
Is 't not the tenour of his oracle,
That King Leontes shall not have an heir
Till his lost child be found? which that it shall,   40
Is all as monstrous to our human reason
As my Antigonus to break his grave
And come again to me; who, on my life,
Did perish with the infant.   'T is your counsel
My lord should to the heavens be contrary,
Oppose against their wills. [*To Leontes*] Care not for
     issue;
The crown will find an heir: great Alexander

Left his to the worthiest; so his súccessor
Was like to be the best.
  *Leon.*      Good Paulina,
Who hast the memory of Hermione,     50
I know, in honour, O that ever I
Had squared me to thy counsel!—then, even now,
I might have look'd upon my queen's full eyes,
Have taken treasure from her lips,—
  *Paul.*      And left them
More rich for what they yielded.
  *Leon.*      Thou speak'st truth.
No more such wives; therefore, no wife: one worse,
And better us'd, would make her sainted spirit
Again possess her corpse, and on this stage,
(Where we offenders now), appear soul-vex'd,
And begin, "Why to me?"
  *Paul.*     Had she such power,  60
She had just cause.
  *Leon.*    She had; and would incense me
To murder her I married.
  *Paul.*      I should so.
Were I the ghost that walk'd, I'd bid you mark
Her eye, and tell me for what dull part in 't
You chose her; then I'd shriek, that even your ears
Should rift to hear me; and the words that follow'd
Should be, "Remember mine."
  *Leon.*      Stars, stars,
And all eyes else dead coals! Fear thou no wife:
I'll have no wife, Paulina.
  *Paul.*     Will you swear
Never to marry but by my free leave?    70
  *Leon.* Never, Paulina; so be blest my spirit!
  *Paul.* Then, good my lords, bear witness to his oath.
  *Cleo.* You tempt him over-much.
  *Paul.*      Unless another,

As like Hermione as is her picture,
Affront his eye.

   *Cleo.*         Good madam,—
   *Paul.*               I have done.
Yet, if my lord will marry,—if you will, sir,
No remedy, but you will,—give me the office
To choose you a queen: she shall not be so young
As was your former; but she shall be such        79
As, walk'd your first queen's ghost, it should take joy
To see her in your arms.

   *Leon.*            My true Paulina,
We shall not marry till thou bidd'st us.

   *Paul.*                That
Shall be when your first queen's again in breath;
Never till then.

*Enter a* Gentleman

   *Gent.* One that gives out himself Prince Florizel,
Son of Polixenes, with his princess, she
The fairest I have yet beheld, desires access
To your high presence.

   *Leon.*         What with him? he comes not
Like to his father's greatness: his approach,
So out of circumstance and sudden, tells us     90
'T is not a visitation fram'd, but forc'd
By need and accident. What train?

   *Gent.*              But few,
And those but mean.

   *Leon.*       His princess, say you, with him?
   *Gent.* Ay, the most peerless piece of earth, I think,
That e'er the sun shone bright on.

   *Paul.*            O Hermione,
As every present time doth boast itself
Above a better gone, so must thy grave
Give way to what 's seen now! Sir, you yourself

Have said and writ so, but your writing now
Is colder than that theme, "She had not been,          100
Nor was not to be equall'd;"—thus your verse
Flow'd with her beauty once: 't is shrewdly ebb'd,
To say you have seen a better.

    *Gent.*               Pardon, madam:
The one I have almost forgot,—your pardon;
The other, when she has obtain'd your eye,
Will have your tongue too.    This is a creature,
Would she begin a sect, might quench the zeal
Of all professors else; make proselytes
Of who she but bid follow.

    *Paul.*             How! not women?

    *Gent.* Women will love her, that she is a woman 110
More worth than any man; men, that she is
The rarest of all women.

    *Leon.*          Go, Cleomenes;
Yourself, assisted with your honour'd friends,
Bring them to our embracement.

                      [*Exeunt Cleomenes and others.*
                      Still, 't is strange
He thus should steal upon us.

    *Paul.*            Had our prince,
Jewel of children, seen this hour, he had pair'd
Well with this lord: there was not full a month
Between their births.

    *Leon.* Prithee, no more; cease; thou know'st
He dies to me again when talk'd of: sure,          120
When I shall see this gentleman, thy speeches
Will bring me to consider that which may
Unfurnish me of reason.    They are come.

    *Re-enter* CLEOMENES *and others, with* FLORIZEL
               *and* PERDITA

Your mother was most true to wedlock, prince;

For she did print your royal father off,
Conceiving you: were I but twenty-one,
Your father's image is so hit in you,
His very air, that I should call you brother,
As I did him, and speak of something wildly
By us perform'd before.    Most dearly welcome!    130
And your fair princess,—goddess!—O, alas!
I lost a couple, that 'twixt heaven and earth
Might have thus stood begetting wonder, as
You, gracious couple, do: and then I lost—
All mine own folly—the society,
Amity too, of your brave father, whom,
Though bearing misery, I desire my life
Once more to look on him.

   *Flo.*              By his command
Have I here touch'd Sicilia, and from him
Give you all greetings that a king, at friend,    140
Can send his brother: and, but infirmity
Which waits upon worn times hath something seiz'd
His wish'd ability, he had himself
The lands and waters 'twixt your throne and his
Measur'd to look upon you; whom he loves—
He bade me say so—more than all the sceptres
And those that bear them living.

   *Leon.*             O my brother.
Good gentleman! the wrongs I have done thee stir
Afresh within me; and these thy offices,
So rarely kind, are as interpreters    150
Of my behindhand slackness!    Welcome hither,
As is the spring to the earth.    And hath he too
Expos'd this paragon to the fearful usage,
At least ungentle, of the dreadful Neptune,
To greet a man not worth her pains, much less
The adventure of her person.

   *Flo.*              Good my lord,

She came from Libya.

  *Leon.*     Where the warlike Smalus,
That noble honour'd lord, is fear'd and lov'd?

  *Flo.* Most royal sir, from thence; from him whose
    daughter
His tears proclaim'd his, parting with her: thence, 160
A prosperous south-wind friendly, we have cross'd,
To execute the charge my father gave me,
For visiting your highness: my best train
I have from your Sicilian shores dismiss'd;
Who for Bohemia bend, to signify
Not only my success in Libya, sir,
But my arrival, and my wife's, in safety
Here where we are.

  *Leon.*    The blessed gods
Purge all infection from our air whilst you
Do climate here!   You have a holy father,  170
A graceful gentleman; against whose person,
So sacred as it is, I have done sin:
For which the heavens, taking angry note,
Have left me issueless; and your father's blest,
As he from heaven merits it, with you,
Worthy his goodness.   What might I have been,
Might I a son and daughter now have look'd on,
Such goodly things as you!

*Enter a* Lord

  *Lord.*     Most noble sir,
That which I shall report will bear no credit,
Were not the proof so nigh.   Please you, great sir, 180
Bohemia greets you from himself by me;
Desires you to attach his son, who has—
His dignity and duty both cast off—
Fled from his father, from his hopes, and with
A shepherd's daughter.

*Leon.*                    Where's Bohemia? speak.

*Lord.* Here in your city; I now came from him:
I speak amazedly; and it becomes
My marvel and my message.   To your court
Whiles he was hastening, in the chase, it seems,
Of this fair couple, meets he on the way          190
The father of this seeming lady and
Her brother, having both their country quitted
With this young prince.

*Flo.*                    Camillo has betray'd me;
Whose honour and whose honesty till now
Endur'd all weathers.

*Lord.*               Lay 't so to his charge:
He 's with the king your father.

*Leon.*                    Who?  Camillo?

*Lord.* Camillo, sir; I spake with him; who now
Has these poor men in question.   Never saw I
Wretches so quake: they kneel, they kiss the earth;
Forswear themselves as often as they speak:          200
Bohemia stops his ears, and threatens them
With divers deaths in death.

*Per.*                    O my poor father!
The heaven sets spies upon us, will not have
Our contract celebrated.

*Leon.*                    You are married?

*Flo.* We are not sir, nor are we like to be;
The stars, I see, will kiss the valleys first:
The odds for high and low 's alike.

*Leon.*                              My lord,
Is this the daughter of a king?

*Flo.*                    She is,
When once she is my wife.          209

*Leon.* That "once," I see by your good father's speed,
Will come on very slowly.   I am sorry,
Most sorry, you have broken from his liking,

Where you were tied in duty; and as sorry
Your choice is not so rich in worth as beauty,
That you might well enjoy her.

*Flo.*                              Dear, look up:
Though Fortune, visible an enemy,
Should chase us, with my father, power no jot
Hath she to change our loves.   Beseech you, sir,
Remember since you ow'd no more to time
Than I do now: with thought of such affections,      220
Step forth mine advocate; at your request
My father will grant precious things as trifles.

*Leon.*  Would he do so, I'd beg your precious mistress,
Which he counts but a trifle.

*Paul.*                          Sir, my liege,
Your eye hath too much youth in 't: not a month
'Fore your queen died, she was more worth such gazes
Than what you look on now.

*Leon.*                       I thought of her,
Even in these looks I made.   [*To Florizel*] But your
      petition
Is yet unanswer'd.   I will to your father:
Your honour not o'erthrown by your desires,        230
I am friend to them and you: upon which errand
I now go toward him; therefore follow me,
And mark what way I make: come, good my lord.

                                        [*Exeunt.*

SCENE II.   *Before Leontes' palace*

*Enter* AUTOLYCUS *and a* Gentleman

*Aut.*  Beseech you, sir, were you present at this relation?

*First Gent.*  I was by at the opening of the fardel,
heard the old shepherd deliver the manner how he found
it: whereupon, after a little amazedness, we were all

commanded out of the chamber; only this methought I heard the shepherd say, he found the child.

*Aut.* I would most gladly know the issue of it.          8

*First Gent.* I make a broken delivery of the business; but the changes I perceived in the king and Camillo were very notes of admiration: they seem'd almost, with staring on one another, to tear the cases of their eyes. There was speech in their dumbness, language in their very gesture; they look'd as they had heard of a world ransom'd, or one destroyed: a notable passion of wonder appeared in them; but the wisest beholder, that knew no more but seeing, could not say if the importance were joy or sorrow; but in the extremity of the one it must needs be.          19

*Enter another* Gentleman

Here comes a gentleman that happily knows more. The news, Rogero?

*Sec. Gent.* Nothing but bonfires: the oracle is ful-fill'd; the king's daughter is found: such a deal of wonder is broken out within this hour, that ballad-makers cannot be able to express it.

*Enter a third* Gentleman

Here comes the Lady Paulina's steward: he can deliver you more. How goes it now, sir? this news which is call'd true is so like an old tale, that the verity of it is in strong suspicion: has the king found his heir?          29

*Third Gent.* Most true, if ever truth were pregnant by circumstance: that which you hear you 'll swear you see, there is such unity in the proofs. The mantle of Queen Hermione's, her jewel about the neck of it, the letters of Antigonus found with it which they know to be his character, the majesty of the creature in resem-blance of the mother, the affection of nobleness which nature shows above her breeding, and many other evidences proclaim her with all certainty to be the king's daughter. Did you see the meeting of the two kings?

*Sec. Gent.* No. 40

*Third Gent.* Then have you lost a sight, which was to be seen, cannot be spoken of. There might you have beheld one joy crown another, so and in such manner, that it seem'd sorrow wept to take leave of them, for their joy waded in tears. There was casting up of eyes, holding up of hands, with countenance of such distraction, that they were to be known by garment, not by favour. Our king, being ready to leap outside of himself for joy of his found daughter, as if that joy were now become a loss, cries, "O, thy mother, thy mother!" then asks Bohemia forgiveness; then embraces his son-in-law; then again worries he his daughter with clipping her; now he thanks the old shepherd, which stands by like a weather-bitten conduit of many kings' reigns. I never heard of such another encounter, which lames report to follow it and undoes description to do it. 57

*Sec. Gent.* What, pray you, became of Antigonus, that carried hence the child?

*Third Gent.* Like an old tale still, which will have matter to rehearse, though credit be asleep and not an ear open. He was torn to pieces with a bear: this avouches the shepherd's son; who has not only his innocence, which seems much, to justify him, but a handkerchief and rings of his that Paulina knows. 65

*First Gent.* What became of his bark and his followers?

*Third Gent.* Wrackt the same instant of their master's death and in the view of the shepherd: so that all the instruments which aided to expose the child were even then lost when it was found. But O, the noble combat

that 'twixt joy and sorrow was fought in Paulina! She
had one eye declin'd for the loss of her husband, another
elevated that the oracle was fulfill'd: she lifted the
princess from the earth; and so locks her in embracing,
as if she would pin her to her heart that she might no
more be in danger of losing.                    77

*First Gent.* The dignity of this act was worth the
audience of kings and princes, for by such was it acted.

*Third Gent.* One of the prettiest touches of all, and
that which angl'd for mine eyes, caught the water though
not the fish, was when, at the relation of the queen's
death, with the manner how she came to 't bravely
confess'd and lamented by the king, how attentiveness
wounded his daughter; till, from one sign of dolour to
another, she did, with an "Alas," I would fain say,
bleed tears, for I am sure my heart wept blood. Who
was most marble there changed colour; some swooned,
all sorrowed: if all the world could have seen 't, the woe
had been universal.                    90

*First Gent.* Are they returned to the court?

*Third Gent.* No: the princess hearing of her mother's
statue, which is in the keeping of Paulina,—a piece
many years in doing, and now newly perform'd by that
rare Italian master, Julio Romano, who, had he himself
eternity and could put breath into his work, would
beguile Nature of her custom, so perfectly he is her ape:
he so near to Hermione hath done Hermione, that they
say one would speak to her and stand in hope of answer:
—thither with all greediness of affection are they gone;
and there they intend to sup.                    101

*Sec. Gent.* I thought she had some great matter there
in hand; for she hath privately twice or thrice a day,
ever since the death of Hermione, visited that removed
house. Shall we thither, and with our company piece
the rejoicing?

*First Gent.* Who would be thence that has the benefit of access? every wink of an eye, some new grace will be born: our absence makes us unthrifty to our knowledge. Let's along.          [*Exeunt Gentlemen.*

*Aut.* Now, had I not the dash of my former life in me, would preferment drop on my head. I brought the old man and his son aboard the prince; told him I heard them talk of a fardel and I know not what: but he at that time, over-fond of the shepherd's daughter, so he then took her to be, who began to be much sea-sick, and himself little better, extremity of weather continuing, this mystery remained undiscover'd. But 't is all one to me; for had I been the finder-out of this secret, it would not have relish'd among my other discredits. 120

*Enter* Shepherd *and* Clown

Here comes those I have done good to against my will, and already appearing in the blossoms of their fortune.

*Shep.* Come, boy; I am past moe children, but thy sons and daughters will be all gentlemen born.

*Clo.* You are well met, sir. You deni'd to fight with me this other day, because I was no gentleman born. See you these clothes? say you see them not and think me still no gentleman born: you were best say these robes are not gentlemen born: give me the lie, do, and try whether I am not now a gentleman born. 132

*Aut.* I know you are now, sir, a gentleman born.

*Clo.* Ay, and have been so any time these four hours.

*Shep.* And so have I, boy.

*Clo.* So you have: but I was a gentleman born before my father; for the king's son took me by the hand, and call'd me brother; and then the two kings call'd my father brother; and then the prince my brother and the princess my sister called my father father; and so we wept, and there was the first gentleman-like tears that ever we shed.                                                                        142

*Shep.* We may live, son, to shed many more.

*Clo.* Ay; or else 't were hard luck, being in so preposterous estate as we are.

*Aut.* I humbly beseech you, sir, to pardon me all the faults I have committed to your worship, and to give me your good report to the prince my master.

*Shep.* Prithee, son, do; for we must be gentle, now we are gentlemen.                                                             150

*Clo.* Thou wilt amend thy life?

*Aut.* Ay, an it like your good worship.

*Clo.* Give me thy hand: I will swear to the prince thou art as honest a true fellow as any is in Bohemia.

*Shep.* You may say it, but not swear it.

*Clo.* Not swear it, now I am a gentleman? Let boors and franklins say it, I'll swear it.

*Shep.* How if it be false, son?                                              158

*Clo.* If it be ne'er so false, a true gentleman may swear it in the behalf of his friend: and I'll swear to the prince thou art a tall fellow of thy hands and that thou wilt not be drunk; but I know thou art no tall fellow of thy hands and that thou wilt be drunk: but I'll swear it, and I would thou wouldst be a tall fellow of thy hands.                                                               165

*Aut.* I will prove so, sir, to my power.

*Clo.* Ay, by any means prove a tall fellow: if I do not wonder how thou dar'st venture to be drunk, not being a tall fellow, trust me not. Hark! the kings and the princes, our kindred, are going to see the queen's picture. Come, follow us: we'll be thy good masters.

*[Exeunt.*

SCENE III.    *A Chapel in Paulina's house*

*To Hermione, like a statue, curtained, enter* LEONTES,
     POLIXENES, FLORIZEL, PERDITA, CAMILLO, PAULINA,
     Lords, *and* Attendants.

*Leon.*  O grave and good Paulina, the great comfort
That I have had of thee!
     *Paul.*                     What, sovereign sir,
I did not well, I meant well.   All my services
You have paid home: but that you have vouchsaf'd
With your crown'd brother and these your contracted
Heirs of your kingdoms, my poor house to visit,
It is a surplus of your grace, which never
My life may last to answer.
     *Leon.*                    O Paulina,
We honour you with trouble: but we came
To see the statue of our queen: your gallery          10
Have we pass'd through, not without much content
In many singularities; but we saw not
That which my daughter came to look upon,
The statue of her mother.
     *Paul.*                    As she liv'd peerless,
So her dead likeness, I do well believe,
Excels whatever yet you look'd upon
Or hand of man hath done; therefore I keep it
Lonely, apart.   But here it is: prepare
To see the life as lively mock'd as ever
Still sleep mock'd death: behold, and say 't is well.     20
          [*Paulina draws back a curtain, and discovers
                  Hermione standing like a statue.*
I like your silence, it the more shows off
Your wonder: but yet speak; first, you, my liege:
Comes it not something near?
     *Leon.*                    Her natural posture!

Chide me, dear stone, that I may say indeed
Thou art Hermione; or rather, thou art she
In thy not chiding, for she was as tender
As infancy and grace.   But yet, Paulina,
Hermione was not so much wrinkled, nothing
So aged as this seems.

   *Pol.*                    O, not by much.

   *Paul.* So much the more our carver's excellence;   3c
Which lets go by some sixteen years and makes her
As she liv'd now.

   *Leon.*          As now she might have done
So much to my good comfort, as it is
Now piercing to my soul.   O, thus she stood,
Even with such life of majesty, warm life,
As now it coldly stands, when first I woo'd her!
I am ashamed: does not the stone rebuke me
For being more stone than it?   O royal piece,
There's magic in thy majesty, which has
My evils conjur'd to remembrance, and               40
From thy admiring daughter took the spirits,
Standing like stone with thee!

   *Per.*                And give me leave,
And do not say 't is superstition, that
I kneel and then implore her blessing.   Lady,
Dear queen, that ended when I but began,
Give me that hand of yours to kiss.

   *Paul.*                O, patience!
The statue is but newly fix'd, the colour's
Not dry.

   *Cam.* My lord, your sorrow was too sore laid on,
Which sixteen winters cannot blow away,             50
So many summers dry: scarce any joy
Did ever so long live; no sorrow
But kill'd itself much sooner.

   *Pol.*                Dear my brother,

Let him that was the cause of this have power
To take off so much grief from you as he
Will piece up in himself.

*Paul.*                    Indeed, my lord,
If I had thought the sight of my poor image
Would thus have wrought you, for the stone is mine,
I 'd not have show'd it.

*Leon.*                    Do not draw the curtain.    59

*Paul.* No longer shall you gaze on 't, lest your fancy
May think anon it moves.

*Leon.*                    Let be, let be.
Would I were dead, but that, methinks, already—
What was he that did make it?   See, my lord,
Would you not deem it breath'd? and that those veins
Did verily bear blood?

*Pol.*                    Masterly done:
The very life seems warm upon her lip.

*Leon.* The fixure of her eye has motion in 't,
As we are mock'd with art.

*Paul.*                    I 'll draw the curtain:
My lord 's almost so far transported, that
He 'll think anon it lives.

*Leon.*                    O sweet Paulina,    70
Make me to think so twenty years together!
No settled senses of the world can match
The pleasure of that madness.   Let 't alone.

*Paul.* I am sorry, sir, I have thus far stirr'd you: but
I could afflict you further.

*Leon.*                    Do, Paulina;
For this affliction has a taste as sweet
As any cordial comfort.   Still, methinks,
There is an air comes from her: what fine chisel
Could ever yet cut breath?   Let no man mock me,
For I will kiss her.

*Paul.*                    Good my lord, forbear:    80

The ruddiness upon her lip is wet;
You'll mar it if you kiss it, stain your own
With oily painting.    Shall I draw the curtain?

   *Leon.*  No, not these twenty years.

   *Per.*                   So long could I
Stand by, a looker on.

   *Paul.*             Either forbear,
Quit presently the chapel, or resolve you
For more amazement.   If you can behold it,
I'll make the statue move indeed, descend
And take you by the hand: but then you'll think—
Which I protest against—I am assisted        90
By wicked powers.

   *Leon.*          What you can make her do,
I am content to look on: what to speak,
I am content to hear; for 't is as easy
To make her speak as move.

   *Paul.*               It is requir'd
You do awake your faith.   Then all stand still;
On: those that think it is unlawful business
I am about, let them depart.

   *Leon.*            Proceed:
No foot shall stir.

   *Paul.*         Music, awake her; strike!   [*Music.*
'T is time; descend; be stone no more; approach;
Strike all that look upon with marvel.   Come;    100
I'll fill your grave up: stir: nay, come away;
Bequeath to death your numbness, for from him
Dear life redeems you.—You perceive she stirs:
                [*Hermione steps from her pedestal.*
Start not; her actions shall be holy as
You hear my spell is lawful: do not shun her,
Until you see her die again; for then
You kill her double.   Nay, present your hand:
When she was young you woo'd her; now in age

Is she become the suitor?

    *Leon.*               O, she's warm!

If this be magic, let it be an art          110

Lawful as eating.

    *Pol.*          She embraces him.

    *Cam.* She hangs about his neck:

If she pertain to life, let her speak too.

    *Pol.* Ay, and make 't manifest where she has liv'd,

Or how stol'n from the dead.

    *Paul.*          That she is living,

Were it but told you, should be hooted at

Like an old tale: but it appears she lives,

Though yet she speak not.   Mark a little while.

Please you to interpose, fair madam: kneel    119

And pray your mother's blessing.   Turn, good lady;

Our Perdita is found.

    *Her.*          You gods, look down,

And from your sacred vials pour your graces

Upon my daughter's head!   Tell me, mine own,

Where hast thou been preserv'd? where liv'd? how

      found

Thy father's court? for thou shalt hear that I,

Knowing by Paulina that the oracle

Gave hope thou wast in being, have preserv'd

Myself to see the issue.

    *Paul.*         There's time enough for that;

Lest they desire upon this push to trouble

Your joys with like relation.   Go together,    130

You precious winners all; your exultation

Partake to every one.   I, an old turtle,

Will wing me to some wither'd bough, and there

My mate, that's never to be found again,

Lament till I am lost.

    *Leon.*         O, peace, Paulina!

Thou shouldst a husband take by my consent,

As I by thine a wife: this is a match,
And made between 's by vows.   Thou hast found mine;
But how, is to be question'd; for I saw her,
As I thought, dead; and have in vain said many        140
A prayer upon her grave.   I'll not seek far,—
For him, I partly know his mind,—to find thee
An honourable husband.   Come, Camillo,
And take her by the hand, whose worth and honesty
Is richly noted and here justified
By us, a pair of kings.   Let 's from this place.
What! look upon my brother: both your pardons,
That e'er I put between your holy looks
My ill suspicion.   This is your son-in-law,
And son unto the king, whom heavens directing,        150
Is troth plight to your daughter.   Good Paulina,
Lead us from hence; where we may leisurely
Each one demand and answer to his part
Perform'd in this wide gap of time, since first
We were dissever'd: hastily lead away.        [*Exeunt*.

# NOTES

---

## Act I—Scene 1

A preliminary scene, consisting merely of conversation, without action. (Contrast the opening scene of the nearly contemporary *Tempest*—a life and death emergency with the attendant intensity and rapidity.) The conversation serves to initiate us into the general situation: the visit of the Bohemian king to Sicily, the old friendship of the two kings, and the elaborate politeness, touched with a prophetic suggestion of hollowness, which prevails between the two courts.

1. **Bohemia.** To save Shakespeare's geography Hanmer read throughout the play " Bithynia ".

6. **Bohemia,** the King of Bohemia (not as in l. 1 the country). So Sicilia, l. 21, &c. Similarly, " England " is the English king in *King John, Henry V, Macbeth*; " France ", the French king (historical or fictitious), in *All's Well, King John, Henry V, King Lear.*

8. The Folio has a colon after *shame us,* making the two clauses independent sentences. But this makes the sequence of the second exceedingly abrupt. Harsh concision is not Archidamus's foible. The Cambridge editions rightly omit the stop.

11. **in the freedom of my knowledge,** with the assurance of one who knows the truth. In the ensuing sentence Archidamus's assurance does not avail to provide him with a sufficiency of courtly phrases.

13. **We will give you,** &c. The euphuistic balance of the sentence, as well as its pretentiously learned words, are proper to a speech of courtly compliment.

21 f. Camillo's description of the lifelong and intimate friendship between the two kings has, in retrospect, the effect of unconscious irony. It heightens our sense of the shallowness of Leontes, who can imagine himself betrayed by such a friend.

    **over-kind,** too kind. An excess of kindness is between them, impossible.

23. **such . . . which,** such as (a common Elizabethan idiom).

27. **royally attorneyed,** performed by representatives in a manner worthy of kings.

29. **a vast,** an immense expanse of sea. So Pericles on shipboard in the storm, "Thou god of this great vast" (*Pericles*, iii. 1. 1). It was applied also to any other space without apparent bounds, as that of the night sky. "In the dead vast and middle of the night" (*Hamlet*, i. 2. 198).

32. **I think not, &c.** Archidamus's assurance implies that those who surround Leontes are completely unprepared for the affair which wrecks "their loves", notwithstanding that Polixenes has been for nine months a guest at his court (i. 2. 1).

35. **into my note,** under my observation.

37. **physics the subject,** acts like a medicine on the sufferings of the people.

## Scene 2

This great scene, which not only starts the action but prepares the whole action of the first three acts, is a striking example of the swift and slightly motived changes characteristic of the plots of the "Romances". It consists of three sub-scenes, with links of subordinate dialogue. The first (1–193) carries us through the whole gamut of moods from Leontes's urgent but vain entreaties to his guest to stay, successfully reinforced with exquisite charm by his wife, to the first indication of his mad suspicion (108) and its violent explosion (186) after their departure. In the second sub-scene Camillo hears it with incredulous amazement, but finally consents unwillingly to "remove" Polixenes by poison. In the third, confronted by Polixenes himself, Camillo is overcome by his palpable innocence, resolves to throw in his lot with him, discloses the king's plot, and arranges for the instant departure of both. The demeanour of Polixenes and Camillo, in the face of the king's charge, like that of Hermione herself, convinces us of Leontes's moral isolation, and that he could do nothing but for his royal power.

1. **the watery star,** the moon, chief source of the tides. The shepherd has seen nine months pass since, &c. The duration of Polixenes's visit to the Sicilian court is thus defined to give superficial plausibility to the king's repudiation of his child (ii. 3).

6. **like a cipher, &c.** No amount of words could express the measure of our gratitude or cancel our debt; I therefore say simply "We thank you" to imply all the thanks unsaid, as a "nought" added to a figure multiplies all that precedes.

8. **moe,** more; originally the adverbial form (O.E. *mā*) used in Elizabethan English of number, as *more* of size.

12. **that may blow, &c.;** dependent on "fears".

13. **sneaping**, nipping. Polixenes fears that, on his return, he may find the anxious forebodings he has expressed ("put forth") justified. The phrase glances also at the premature putting forth of buds in spring, but this is not the real point, and Hanmer was wrong in proposing to read "early" for "truly".

16. **Than you can put us to 't**, than to succumb to any trial you can make of us (by demands on our hospitality). "To put to 't", in Elizabethan English, is regularly "to put to the test". E.g. "they have a leader that will put you (the Roman soldiery) to 't" (*Coriolanus*, i. 1. 233).

18. **'s**, contraction for "us", used only where this is unemphatic.

24. **even**. This word is used in many shades of meaning in Elizabethan English Here it does not contrast "dragging" with a more moderate compulsion, but stamps "dragging" as a literally true, not figurative, description of his situation. "Just drag me." Cf. Bradley on the Elizabethan English uses of this word (*Shakespeare's England*, II. 559 *f.*).

25. To hinder my return, even from kind motives, would be to punish me.

28. Hermione's immense superiority to Leontes in brain as in heart is at once evident. She is a fine strategist, and puts herself at once at Polixenes's point of view.

32. **The by-gone day**. "Day" for a long undefined period, as in "our day". Hermione is arguing boldly from the quiet that has prevailed there during Polixenes's visit.

41. **let**, detain.

**gest**, date, properly a stopping-place (Fr. *gîte*) on a journey; hence the time appointed for stopping there.

42. **good deed**, in good deed, an asseveration.

43. **jar**, tick.

44. **What lady she**, any woman of rank. *She* is probably used substantivally, as *he* often is. "I am that he, that unfortunate he" (*As You Like It*, iii. 2. 414).

47. **limber**, slight, easily set aside. "Verily" was not a serious oath.

53. **your fees**. Prisoners were then charged fees for their maintenance, which they had to pay on liberation.

59 f. Hermione, with the most delicate tact, gives a turn to the conversation which at once relieves the strain of Polixenes's unwilling consent. It also enables us to appreciate the old intimacy between the two kings. Hermione's arch wit and badinage are delightful, but her innocent familiarity only serves to give occasion to Leontes's suspicions.

74. Theobald explained this to mean "setting aside the imposition", our heritage of "original sin"; but the word "clear'd" favours the bolder thought that our "not guilty" would have included our "original sin" also.

80. **to boot!** to our help! Similarly, "St. George to boot!" as a cry.

87. **At my request he would not.** This, muttered half to himself, is the first clear hint of Leontes's suspicion.

91 f. In 91–3 Hermione thinks of women's susceptibility to praise as making them "tame" or easily compliant; in 94–6, as stimulating them to effort. When a good deed misses its due praise, a thousand others which depend on that praise remain undone.

96. **heat an acre**, run over a single course or "heat". She probably thinks of one of an acre circuit, about 100 yards.

**But to the goal**, to return to the immediate point. Hermione has digressed to dwell upon the persuasiveness of praise given to women: she now presses her question about the first occasion on which she had earned Leontes's praise. Her phrase falls into the racing figure of the previous clause, but has nothing to do with it.

104. **clap thyself.** To clasp or "shake" hands was the usual accompaniment of the conclusion of a bargain.

106. Hermione, by as it were "bracketing" the two occasions on which she has "spoken well", has innocently fomented Leontes's incipient suspicion; and the distinction she proceeds to draw between husband and friend, clear and final as it is, does not efface the fact that she *compares* them. Her ensuing demonstrations of her friendship seem to continue the dangerous comparison, and his morbid eye interprets the most innocent gestures for the worse.

111. **This entertainment, &c.** Simple unreserve may use action such as this (which may therefore be innocent).

113. **fertile bosom**, expansive emotion, the natural frankness of goodwill.

115. **paddling**, fingering amorously.

118. **The mort, &c.**, the notes sounded on the hunter's horn to announce the death of the deer.

120. **I' fecks**, euphemism for in faith.

121. **bawcock**, a term of endearment for a boy (*beau coq*).

125. **neat**, cattle; a generic term for them all.

**virginalling**, playing with the fingers as on a virginal or spinet.

128. **a rough pash**, a forehead rough with incipient horns.

**132. blacks,** mourning garments, made, to save cost, by dyeing old ones.

**136. welkin,** properly the clouds, but habitually used of the sky; hence 'blue'.

**137. collop;** playing on the proverb: "it is a dear collop that is cut out of thy own flesh".

**138. Affection, &c.** Passion masters a man's inmost thoughts, makes things supposed impossible seem possible, dreams seem real, unrealities seem actual (the real world having here no share whatever in his thought). It is credible, then, that this same passion may lay hold of something of which there is no other warrant ("beyond commission"), but which is yet real, as the speaker's own mental and physical state bears witness. Leontes is confusedly wrestling with two opposed notions about passion: that it blinds and deludes reason, and that it discovers what cool reason fails to see. His infatuation pushes him towards the latter; but he still looks "unsettled" and distraught.

**151. its.** This form, found only in Shakespeare's latest plays, was probably used by him in his final period, when it was becoming usual. But *it* (as possessive) was also current, and was possibly also used by him. It appears in some passages of the Folio, e.g. below, ii. 3. 177.

**154. methoughts,** methought; by mistaken analogy with "methinks". The accurate form is used immediately after by the same speaker.

**160. squash,** properly an unripe pea or bean.

**161. take eggs, &c.** Will you take something of little value instead of the due payment? Will you pocket an affront?

**177. Apparent,** having the nearest and strongest claim.

**178. shall's attend you.** "Us" for "we" occurs six times after "shall" in Shakespeare. It is to be explained as due to a mixture of the idioms "shall we" and "let us" (Jespersen). So "Shall's to the Capitol?" (*Coriolanus*, iv. 6. 148).

**183. neb,** mouth. Leontes sees Hermione's face lifted, in the warmth of her welcome, towards the king's, and imagines that she is offering to kiss him.

**185. Gone already!** It is all over with me; my wife is lost.

**189. hiss me to my grave.** The image of the actor who is hissed off the stage is applied to Leontes, though what is meant is not that he plays his part badly, but that his "part" is one that it is a disgrace to play at all.

**200. came home,** i.e. dragged, instead of gripping the bottom.

**202.** Camillo unintentionally feeds the suspicions of Leontes.

**203. rounding,** whispering. The two words are synonymous.

**205. gust,** taste.

**206.** Camillo's innocently fatal words may be compared with Desdemona's equally innocent pleading for Cassio at the moment when Othello's suspicion is awakened.

**210. thy conceit, &c.** Camillo's fine understanding, like a sponge, takes in matters that would make no impression on the common blocks.

**212. severals,** individuals.

**213. lower messes,** persons of inferior quality, who " sat below the salt " at table.

**223. chamber-councils,** inmost, most private designs.

**228. bide upon 't,** continue. Leontes presses his point home.

**230. hoxes,** houghs, hamstrings, cuts the instep, a treacherous way of disabling instead of by a frontal attack.

**232. grafted in my serious trust,** admitted to intimacy with my most confidential secrets.

**235.** The four types of the bad servant, to one or other of which Leontes assigns Camillo in this paragraph, should be clearly distinguished.

**237. free,** exempt from blame.

**240. puts forth,** exposes itself.

**244.** Camillo refers to cases in which he may have feared to embark upon an action, doubting its success, where the result nevertheless justified it, and gave the lie to his fears. Malone wrongly thought that Shakespeare meant "cry out for the non-performance". In this case Camillo's fears would have been justified.

**252. its.** This neuter possessive for the usual "his" (as elsewhere in this play) is found only in Shakespeare's latest plays. English usage was clearly in transition.

**266. which to reiterate, &c.** Merely to repeat such a charge would be an offence as great as the sin itself, even were it true.

**274. pin and web,** eye disease, perhaps cataract.

**285. hovering temporizer,** a shifty opportunist, one who changes his position, like a weathercock, "as the wind blows".

**287. were my wife's liver, &c.,** if her body were as infected as her mind she would die in one turn of the hour-glass.

**290. like her medal,** as he wears the medallion of her that hangs about his neck.

**294. thrifts,** interests.

295. **undo more doing**; the removal of Polixenes would stop further illicit relations between the pair.

297. **bench'd**, raised to a seat of honour. So the magistrates' places are distinguished from the "meaner forms" on "the Bench".

**worship**, honour.

299 f. Even Leontes clothes his incitement to murder in slightly euphemistic phrases. A wink is properly a closing of the eyes. Cf. *Tempest*, ii. 1. 285:

> "To the perpetual wink for aye might put
> This ancient morsel."

302. **rash**, swift.

307. **I have lov'd thee.** Camillo uses this pronoun, unusual for a subject to a sovereign, as an appeal to Leontes's memory of their old affection. Leontes is intended to be a considerably younger man.

308. **Make that thy question, &c.**, i.e. suggest that there is any doubt about Hermione's dishonour. Leontes is too much incensed at Camillo's obstinate defence of the queen to heed his protestations of love to himself.

310. **appoint**, dress, clothe; as if the "vexation" were something artificial which he could put off or on at will.

313. The verse is technically of four feet only, but its slow movement and weight of reiterated stresses disguise the anomaly.

317. **blench**, deviate from the right path.

318. **fetch off**, i.e. by death.

321. **thereby for sealing, &c.**, furthermore in order to stop any scandalous reports.

340. **All that are his so too**, i.e. he will compel all his servants also to be false to themselves.

345. Since there is no example of such an assassin prospering afterwards, the most utter villain had better in his own interest refrain.

362. **Be intelligent**, explain yourself.

363. **you must**, i.e. explain.

365. **complexions**, disposition, as betrayed by his demeanour and looks (cf. *v.* 431).

366. As this change affects my own position so closely, I cannot but betray my feeling, also, in my looks.

372. Do not credit me with the basilisk's power to kill with a look.

375. **a gentleman**, a man of noble rank.

376. **Equipped** with a learned man's experience.

378. **In whose success, &c.**, our succession from whom is our title to noble rank.

381. **ignorant**, which 'ignores', that is, feigns ignorance.

387. **What incidency of harm, &c.**, what injurious event is about to befall me.

389. **if to be**, if it can be prevented at all.

400. **vice, screw, force.** The image hints at Camillo's sense that Leontes's belief was due to his own violent impulse, without any ground in facts.

403. **his**, i.e. Judas Iscariot's. To share the lot of Judas was a part of old formulas of excommunication.

408. **Swear his thought over, &c.**, try to outswear it, or swear it down, by calling every star to witness; the word *influence* was specifically used of the supposed effects of the stars on earthly affairs.

415. **The standing of his body**, so long as his body lasts.

**How should this grow?** how can this suspicion have arisen?

419. **trunk**, body, Camillo's person, which will accompany the king as a pledge (*impawn'd*) of his good faith.

425. **this discovery**, by my disclosure of this to you.

432. **thy places**, posts of preferment.

435. **This jealousy, &c.** Polixenes humanely explains and excuses the fierceness of Leontes's anger by the peerless quality of the wife, and his old confidence in the friend, by whom he believed himself injured.

440. **Profess'd**, professed friendship (cf. *Julius Cæsar*, i. 2. 77).

442. **Good expedition, &c.** May my swift departure succeed, bringing comfort to the queen (by securing him from Leontes's anger) whose person has helped to give occasion to the king's jealousy, but who in no wise shares her husband's false suspicion. He knows that she believes in the perfect loyalty of his affection.

446. **avoid**, depart.

———————

## Act II—Scene 1

As frequently in Shakespeare (cf. *Julius Cæsar*, ii. i. 100 *f.*), a scene of serious import is preluded by a passage of charming by-play of no apparent relevance. Mamillius, whispering to his mother the "sad tale best for winter", is rudely interrupted by the harsh notes of the actual *Winter's Tale* which is about to separate for ever the mother and son thus for a last moment seen in confidential intimacy. The remainder of the scene carries out, with the violence and suddenness habitual in these "Romance" plots, the consequences, easily to be foreseen, of the flight of Polixenes and Camillo at the end of the previous act. Hermione is hurried off to prison; but the loud and un-reserved protests of the courtiers throw the fatuity of Leontes into yet more glaring prominence and increase our assurance that justice will finally triumph.

**11. Who taught you this?** The First Folio reads "taught ' this", the others "taught this". The former may represent an elided *ye*, but the pronoun is clearly necessary, and accords with the scansion.

**31. Yond crickets shall not hear it,** i.e. yonder court-ladies with their idle chatter. The phrase emphasizes the boy's masculine contempt for them, conveyed in the preceding dia-logue.

**37. censure,** judgment.

**38. Alack for lesser knowledge!** Would that I knew less!

**39. There may be in the cup.** The spider was held to be venomous, but only when it was seen.

**45. hefts,** retchings, heavings.

**50. discover'd,** disclosed and so frustrated.

**51. a pinch'd thing,** tricked, outwitted, as the victim of a plot.

**62. But I'd say he had not.** The conditional "I'd say" does not, of course, mean that Hermione gives only a qualified or doubtful denial to the charge; she simply declares how she would meet a charge which even now she can hardly believe to be seriously made.

**69. her without-door form,** her outward presence.

**71. petty brands,** marks of infamy, trifling in appearance, but no less significant than open disgrace.

**72. O, I am out.** Leontes, in spite of his violent language, is confusedly aware that his charge may be false, as is shown by his mission to the oracle. He betrays his confusion also by this unintended assertion that those who "shrugged", instead of speaking openly of Hermione's character, did so, as calum-niators, to suggest unreal guilt, instead of in "mercy" to veil an actual offence.

**79. replenish'd,** complete.

**82. thou thing, which, &c.** Leontes will not call a woman of the queen's rank the "thing" she really is, lest the mob should be misled by his example to drop polite distinctions and use a like brutal frankness to other persons of high rank.

5*

**90. federary,** ally, accomplice. The word, probably coined by Shakespeare, occurs only here. He elsewhere uses *fedary* (feodary) in the same sense (*Cymbeline*, iii. 2. 21).

**98. The centre,** the earth.

**100. afar off guilty,** in some (however slight) degree guilty, by the mere fact that he speaks for her.

**111.** The attendants hesitate to execute the king's order, another sign of the general resentment excited by his calumny; hence his impatience.

**114. good fools.** The word was used as a term of endearment. So Lear of the dead Cordelia: "and my poor fool is hanged".

**117. this action I now go on,** the charge on the ground of which I am now going to prison (opposed to "come out", above).

**130–1. I'll keep my stables, &c.** Two ideas seem to mingle in Antigonus's protestation: (1) I will treat my wife as I treat my horses and dogs, (2) I will never let her out of my sight. The first dictates the clause "I'll keep my stables", &c.; the second, suggested by this image but not fully in keeping with it, the clause "I'll go in couples with her", and the more explicit assertion of the following line.

**132. Than;** with "no further".

**137. putter-on,** instigator.

**139. land-damn.** The word cannot be certainly explained, and has frequently been supposed corrupt. But Moorman (ed. *Winter's Tale*, ad loc.) quotes from the *Dialect Dictionary* a phrase *landam* for "to abuse with rancour", formerly current in Gloucestershire; and this probably points to the truth.

**144. I do see't and feel't, &c.** Leontes must be supposed at this point to grasp Antigonus's arm (Hanmer), or perhaps to strike his forehead (Johnson). He says, then, that whereas Antigonus is obtuse to Hermione's crime, he himself feels and sees it as acutely as Antigonus feels the pressure of his hand and sees the fingers that produce the feeling. "The instruments that feel" stands by a bold idiom for "the instruments that produce the feeling".

**151. Upon this ground,** in this matter.

**156. Calls not,** calls not for, is independent of.

**164. overture,** disclosure.

**168. touch'd conjecture,** put conjecture, or suspicion, to the test; implying that it proves the suspicion just by putting the fact suspected beyond doubt. For the sense cf. "had touched his spirit and tried his inclination" (*Coriolanus*, ii. 3. 199).

**169. approbation**, proof. The proof was convincing even without ocular evidence.

**174. wild**, rash, inconsiderate. Cf. below: "a wild dedication of yourselves To unpath'd waters" (iv. 4. 560).

**175. Delphos**, Delphi, the seat of the oracle, in Bœotia. The name is probably confused with that of the island of Delos. Both the name and the curious incident itself are taken over from the romance of the scholar Greene, save that he makes the wife, not the husband, send to the oracle.

**177. Of stuff'd sufficiency**, fully adequate powers.

**186. From**, apart from, without access to—a regular Elizabethan sense. Cf. "Thou shalt build *from* men" (i.e. in seclusion from), *Timon of Athens*, iv. 3. 533.

**free**, accessible to everyone, and therefore to be guarded from the supposed "treachery" of Hermione.

**190. raise**, rouse. So, "the villain Jew with outcries raised the duke" (*Merchant of Venice*, ii. 8. 4). We still use this sense in phrases like "raise the country".

## Scene 2

It is characteristic of the "Romance" technique that Paulina, the most forceful person in the play, and, when the frenzy of Leontes has spent itself, the chief controller of its issues, here emerges suddenly and without the least preparation, for the first time. But her first words bring her vividly before us as a woman of natural power and authority, indignant at the fate of her slandered mistress, and bent on plain speech to its author, but biding her time with entire self-control.

**20. As passes colouring**, as outdoes the arts of the painter. They are more bent upon making Hermione's stainless character look black than a painter is to cover his white canvas with colour. The barely hinted figure is not quite coherent, since the process of painting does not involve the "ado" required to make the slander upon Hermione plausible.

**23. on**, as a consequence of.

**30. lunes**, delusions, fits of temporary lunacy. So: "watch his pettish lunes" (*Troilus and Cressida*, ii. 3. 140), of the no less dangerous moods of Achilles.

**44. free**, generous.

**47. presently**, immediately, the invariable Elizabethan sense.

**49. hammered of this design**, her mind was urgently possessed by it. The word is used in Shakespeare of strong and persistent desires or intentions entertained but not yet urged. So of Antonio's project for sending his son Proteus to see the world, "whereon this month I have been hammering" (*Two Gentlemen of Verona*, i. 3. 18).

50. **tempt**, try, solicit.

55. **come something nearer**; as in *v.* 47 she had invited Paulina to come into the next room.

57. **pass it**, let it pass.

63. **If any be**, i.e. any "trespass". Paulina by this clause guards against the inference, suggested by the phrase "the trespass", that she admits the queen's guilt.

### Scene 3

The tragic plot moves towards its climax with the swiftness usual in the Romances; Paulina is repelled, and the new-born child condemned to the fire. But in keeping with the same "Romantic" technique, the edge of the tragic menace is turned in this very scene; Leontes consents to sentence the child, instead of being destroyed, to be cast away in a "desert place" where "chance", as every reader of Romance knows will cause it to be found and reared; and at the close the messengers from "Delphos" return with Apollo's decree, their unexampled speed (*v.* 197) reflecting their eager hope that the divine voice would destroy the groundless calumny. Paulina's demeanour to Leontes is admirably free from mere rudeness, on the one side, and from any regard for the "divinity (which) doth hedge a king", but which the king himself has so grossly violated, on the other. Such scenes are rare in Shakespeare, as they were in Elizabethan and other royal experience. Kent vainly stemming the passion of Lear is parallel; but Kent is far less collected and resourceful than Paulina, and Leontes quails as Lear never does.

4. **harlot**, vagabond, rascal. The word was applied both to men and, in the special sense of "lewd", to women. It now survives only in the latter sense, and as a noun.

5. **out of the blank and level.** The figure is from shooting, the "blank" being the white centre of the target, the "level" the range of the missile (without any implication that it is fired horizontally). So: "not a heart which in his level came" (*A Lover's Complaint*, 309). Notice the swift transitions from one figure to another in the king's vehement speech: "beyond my arm" suggests physical capture; "out of the blank . . .", shooting down from a distance; "hook to me", grappling an enemy's ship.

17. **solely**, sole, alone. Similarly "left heir to all his lands" (*Taming of the Shrew*, ii. 1. 118).

18. **of him**, i.e. of Polixenes.

20. **Recoil**, attracted to the plural by the immediately preceding "revenges".

30. **free**, innocent; so "make mad the guilty and appal the free" (*Hamlet*, ii. 2. 537).

37. **medicinal**, pronounced "méd'cinal".

41. **gossips**, sponsors at baptism (for the new-born child).

49. **Commit me for committing**; a play upon the two senses of the word, to "arrest" and to "perform".

56. **comforting**, encouraging, countenancing.

60. **make her good**, &c., establish her goodness.

61. **the worst**, i.e. the poorest fighter.

67. **mankind**, masculine, masterful, rudely despotic. Cf. "a plaguy, mankind girl", and "'twas a sound knock she gave me, the mankind girl" (Fletcher, *Monsieur Thomas*). Leontes thus affects to explain his helpless cowering before Paulina's resolute will and scarcely concealed indignation.

68. **intelligencing**, spying, carrying secret information.

74. **woman-tir'd**, henpecked. "Tire" was properly used of birds of prey tearing flesh with their beaks. So "will like an empty eagle tire on the flesh of me" (*1 Henry VI*, i. 1. 269). Hence figuratively.

**unroosted**, driven from your perch.

75. **dame Partlet**; the name of the hen in the English story of *Reynard the Fox* (as in Chaucer's *Nun's Priest's Tale*). It was current as a jocular term for a wife of vigorous character in Shakespeare's time. There is some irony in Falstaff's address to Mrs. Quickly as "Dame Partlet the Hen" (*1 Henry IV*, iii. 3. 60).

78. **forced baseness**, the slur of bastardy violently and unjustly put upon it.

90. **callat**, a lewd woman.

96. **the old proverb**. Staunton quotes from Overbury's *Characters* ("A Sargeant"), 1614: "The devil calls him his white Sonne; he is so like him that hee is the worse for it, and hee looks after [resembles] his father."

100. **trick**, characteristic trait. Cf. "(the fox) will have a wild trick of his ancestors" (*1 Henry IV*, v. 2. 11).

106. **No yellow**; the colour of jealousy.

108. **lozel**, rogue.

123. The reluctant courtiers at length make a show of expelling Paulina.

139. **proper**, own.

153. **I am a feather**, &c.  Leontes naïvely betrays the weakness of conviction and will which underlies his violence.

161. **this beard**, i.e. his own.  Doubts have been raised on the ground that Leontes, who has implied that he is twenty-three years older than his boy Mamillius (i. 2. 154, *f.*), can be little more than thirty years old.

163. **undergo**, undertake.

169. **fail**, failure.  So: "by this my issue's fail" (below, v. i. 27).  "Failure" is not found in Shakespeare.

177. **its**; see note to i. 2. 151.

181. **commend**, commit.

**strangely**, as an alien (which Leontes believes or affects to believe it to be).

188. **be prosperous**, &c., i.e. than this act deserves.

192. **loss**.  The substantive is now regularly, and was then more commonly, applied to cases where the "loser" misses, or is deprived of, some actual or prospective possession, not to those in which he is himself, as we still say, "lost".

197. **account**, reckoning.

---

## Act III—Scene 1

The messengers sent to consult the oracle are now on their way home, bearing Apollo's response in a sealed packet.  They are still full of the wonderful and "unearthly" impression made by the temple and its ceremonies; and while hoping fervently for Hermione's acquittal, are confident that the oracular reply will be "something rare" in any case; for Hermione's guilt, divinely attested, would be an even greater prodigy than the king's infatuation.

2. **the isle**, "Delphos", a then current confusion, as already stated, between the island of Delos, in the Ægean, also sacred to Apollo, and Delphi, on the mainland of Greece, the seat of his world-famous oracle and temple.

8. **burst**, explosive outbreak of speech.  So, of Cloten, "the snatches in his voice and bursts of speaking" (*Cymbeline*, iv. 2. 106).

17. **carriage**, management.  The proclamations, though a "forcible" measure, would at least accelerate the decision.

20. **discover**, disclose.

21. **fresh horses**.  This would naturally imply that they are at least one stage removed both from the port of landing in

Sicily and from their destination, the court; also that the court-city was not itself on the sea-board. But it is hazardous to draw any geographical or historical conclusions whatever in the Romances.

## Scene 2

The trial scene should be compared with that in the slightly later *Henry VIII* (ii. 4). The two noble queens, impeached by their royal husbands (Leontes in blind fatuity, Henry "stung by conscience") bear themselves with equal dignity. The scene is a striking example of the "surprise" technique of the Romances. Hermione's noble self-defence, as fine in its kind as Othello's before the Venetian senati, culminates in a heart-broken cry for death, when she hears her new-born child's fate. But she cares for her honour though not for her life, and appeals to the decision of the oracle. The god's emphatic declaration of her innocence is the turning-point of the plot. The king resists for a moment; but, immediately after, the death of Mamillius is announced; Hermione faints and is carried out, Leontes surrenders without reserve, and abjectly implores pardon from the god. Then Paulina rushes in, and pours upon the king a torrent of grief and anger. But the first sign of his repentance abruptly checks its flow (see note on *v.* 219), and she humbly asks pardon for her feminine rashness and folly.

**16. pretence**, design. Cf. "to keep your great pretences veiled" (*Coriolanus*, i. 2. 20). Though often used as at present, the word could still bear also, as in French, the original sense of something projected, planned, without any suggestion of deceit.

**36. owe**, own, rightfully claim as mine.

**40. for life, &c.** Life is henceforth for Hermione only grief, and she will part with it as readily; whereas her honour concerns her children, who will survive her.

**47. With what encounter so uncurrent, &c.** The only difficult word in this passage is "strained", which must be understood as equivalent to "swerved aside from propriety". "Uncurrent encounter" denotes any unseemly mode of intercourse. Hermione asks, then, simply, in what way her relations with Polixenes have so infringed propriety as to justify her public arraignment.

**53. wanted less.** An example of the double negative still common in Elizabethan English, the negative notion inherent in *want* being fortified by that of *less*, where logic would demand "more".

**56. due**, applicable. For the situation, cf. Rosalind's retort to Ferdinand (who has called her a traitor, because she is "her father's daughter)":

" Treason is not inherited, my lord!
Or, if we did derive it from our friends,
What 's that to me? my father was no traitor!"
*(As You Like It*, i. 3. 63.)

**57. More than mistress of, &c.** I must not acknowledge
myself guilty of faults imputed to me for which I am not
answerable. The construction is elliptical, and only to be
paralleled in the latest plays. " More than mistress of " stands
for " conduct exceeding what I have myself committed ", and
is virtually subject to " which . . . fault ", i.e. which is charged
against me. No opposition is intended between " fault " and
" these bolder vices " (*v.* 53).

**78. level**; see note to ii. 3. 5–6.

**82. fact**, crime; adultresses like you.

**83. concerns more than avails**, gives you useless trouble.

**84. like to itself, &c.** It being the natural and proper fate
of a child whose father is unknown to be " cast out ", this
" brat " is simply, as it were, conforming to type in being so
treated.

**89. bug**, idle terror (" bogey ", " bugbear ").

**90. commodity**, advantage.

**96. Starr'd**, fated.

**97. its**; see note to i. 2. 151. All the Folios here print *it*, the
form actually current for a time during the transition from *his*
to *its*, and possibly written by Shakespeare.

**98. post.** Posts set up in the street were used for the dis-
play of proclamations. They were especially placed before the
houses of the sheriffs (cf. *Twelfth Night*, i. 5. 157).

**99. immodest**, extravagant, passing all bounds.

**106. no life**, it is no question of my life, do not imagine me
to be pleading for that. The construction is again elliptical
but most expressive. Hermione is too eager to repel the idea
that she is asking for life to heed exact syntax. Cf. *v.* 40–3
above.

**116. The emperor of Russia was my father.** In Greene's
romance he is not the father of Bellaria (= Hermione) but of
the wife of Egistus (= Polixenes). The transfer was doubtless
deliberate, her father's former greatness and subsequent death
adding to the pathos of Hermione's situation. It is likely that
both Greene and Shakespeare were thinking of the contemporary Tsar of Muscovy, Ivan the Terrible, one of the most
formidable potentates of the sixteenth century, since he had
excited notoriety at the English court by his mission to England
to obtain the hand of one of Elizabeth's maids of honour as his
consort. His envoys are chaffingly glanced at in *Love's Labour's*

*Lost.* The plan fell through, Elizabeth s and Ivan's notions of a marriage dowry proving by no means to coincide. It may be added that in the interim between Greene's romance (published 1588) and the present play, Ivan had actually died (1598). There is of course no reason whatever to suppose that Shakespeare alluded in any way to Ivan, whose known disposition towards offenders was notoriously at variance with that ascribed by Hermione to her father below (*v.* 118).

**119. flatness,** completeness; the sense of "unqualified" is still current in the adjective ("flat perjury", *Much Ado About Nothing,* iv. 2. 44, &c., "that's flat", i.e. absolutely true); the substantive in this (or any other) sense is not used elsewhere by Shakespeare.

**with eyes of pity, not revenge.** Hermione expresses the merciful attitude towards evildoers characteristic of "Romances" in its extremest form, for the evildoer has not yet either repented (like Iachimo) or been convicted (like Caliban and his associates).

**131. live without an heir.** The later editions of Greene's romance from 1607 onwards (i.e. after his death) substitute *die* for *live.* Shakespeare clearly had the original edition before him. Perdita ("that which is lost") is formally described as his heir (with Florizel) in v. 3. 6.

**139. to report it,** for reporting it.

**140. mere conceit of the queen's speed,** from merely imagining what may happen to the queen. For *conceit* cf. *conceiving,* also applied to Mamillius, ii. 3. 13 above. *Speed* is properly *good* fortune, the word being in origin a verbal noun from the O.E. verb *spówan,* to prosper (like *seed* from *sówan,* to sow, *deed* from *dón, gleed* from *glówan,* &c.). A play between this and the commoner sense "swiftness" provides a pun in *Cymbeline,* iii. 5. 167.

**142. Leontes's sudden surrender,** after his defiance six lines before, again exemplifies the abrupt changes characteristic of the technique of the "Romances".

**161. Not doing it and being done;** i.e. "death" in the one case, "reward" in the other: an example of Shakespeare's later elliptical manner.

**163. Unclasp'd my practice,** disclosed my treacherous plan. "Practice" has often, like "plot", a bad sense; e.g. "sworn unto the practices of France (the French king) to kill us here" (*Henry V,* ii. 2. 90). Cf. "fact", meaning a criminal act.

**166. No richer than his honour,** with only his honour for riches.

**167. Through,** pronounced "thorough". The preposition was common in this disyllabic form, though still habitually written

"through". This spelling is retained in many passages of the
First Folio, where, as here, the metre requires the disyllabic
form. So "And *through* this distemperature we see The seasons
alter" (*Midsummer-Night's Dream*, ii. 1. 106). This pronunciation of the preposition was growing obsolete at the end of
Shakespeare's life, and the later Folios usually substitute the
monosyllable, often adding a word to complete the verse; so
here "through my *dark* rust" (Ff. 2–4).

180. **were but spices of it**, gave merely a "taste" of it,
a small but characteristic portion. Cf. "he hath spices of them
all, not all" (*Coriolanus*, iv. 7. 46).

182. **of a fool.** The phrase carries on the thought of the
two lines before; his betrayal of Polixenes was culpable enough,
but still a "foolery"; the fickleness and ingratitude they showed
were those of a weak, not of a malignant brain. "Of a fool"
with idiomatic brevity conveys this distinction; it means, then,
"in a fool's way" rather than "for a fool".

183. **damnable**, adverbial usage, for "damnably". The
adverb in O.E. was normally formed from the adjective by the
addition of *-e*, though *-lice* (*-ly*) was also frequent. In M.E.
the *-e* was lost, when the adjectival and adverbial forms became
identical. This equivalence was then extended to words of
French or Latin origin, and this usage, though obsolescent,
still survived when Shakespeare wrote.

205. **stir**, remove.

208. **still**, continuously.

214. Paulina's sudden relenting, at the first sign of Leontes's
recognition of the wrong, again exemplifies the "surprise"
technique of the later plays. Contrast Hamlet's merciless
persistence in his chastisement of the queen after she has
owned her guilt with horror (*v.* 90); *Hamlet*, iii. 4, 40 *f*.

219–20. **do not receive affliction At my petition.** She
withdraws her summons to him to betake himself "to nothing
but despair".

236. **my recreation**; i.e. weeping will be for him what
amusement is to other men. Not "restoration" (Arden edition),
of which Leontes is not thinking.


## Scene 3

This scene distinctly resembles in topic various scenes of
the other Romances—the storm-scene in *The Tempest*, the
hunting-scene in *Cymbeline*—but has no pretensions to dramatic
quality. The fate of Antigonus is too unrelated to his character or actions to be tragic, too sudden and casual to be even
moving; and for a modern audience it comes dangerously near

to undesigned comedy—a lapse even in the confessedly loose Romance technique. The harrowing details later provided do not alter the case. The prose dialogue between the Shepherd and the Clown which follows is Elizabethan common form, but has scarcely any distinctively Shakespearean touch.

1. **perfect**, certain, knowing beyond doubt. Cf. "I am perfect that the Pannonians are now in arms" (*Cymbeline*, iii. 1. 73); "What hast thou done? I am perfect what" (*ibid.* iv. 2. 118).

12. **this place is famous**, &c. This is Antigonus's (and our) only warning of his coming fate.

21. **vessel**. The figure is partly suggested by the biblical "the weaker vessel", but is not confined to women (cf. "Now is that noble vessel full of grief", of Brutus, *Julius Cæsar*, v. 5. 13).

22. **becoming**, seemly. The word, odd at first sight in the context, is suggested by the following rather than by the previous clause: Antigonus's thought has already passed from the tears to the "purity and sanctity" of the apparition. On the supposition that the word should carry on the figure of the filled vessel, various needless emendations have been proposed— "o'er-running", "o'er-brimming", "beteeming" (outpouring).

41. **squared**, regulated. Cf. below, "squared me to thy counsel", v. 1. 52.

44. **it should here be laid**, &c. Antigonus is thus made deliberately to leave the child in the land of its reputed father. Shakespeare has thus diminished the play of chance in the connexion of the two parts of his plot. In Greene the exposed child's fate is committed to, and determined by, "Fortune" alone.

47. **thy character**, the written account of the babe and its origin.

**there these.** "These" are the ornaments, &c., discovered by the Clown below.

48. **pretty**; as substantive, a colloquial use. Only once elsewhere (doubtfully) in Shakespeare: "I post unto my pretty" (*The Passionate Pilgrim*, 201).

**both breed thee, . . . and still rest thine.** Antigonus may be supposed to mean either that the ornaments would be more than enough to pay for Perdita's rearing, or that, as a token of her high birth, they would induce her lowly discoverers to bring her up in the hope of reward, while remaining her possession.

51. **loss and what may follow.** "Loss" could mean "destruction", as above in ii. 3. 191. But the word expressed directly only the severance or casting away, not the death

which might follow. Hence Antigonus can here distinguish between the child's exposure and its possible consequences.

**56. A savage clamour.** The warning of the Mariner in *v.* 10 is suddenly fulfilled. Antigonus discovers that what he took to be the exposure of a child is also a hunt, in which he is the quarry, and rushes for the ship. But he sees that escape is vain, and gives himself up for lost.

This is the only death in Shakespeare which justly provokes us. Its evident object, to relieve the play of a person who has no further function in it, is effected in a way epic rather than dramatic. The suddenness of the catastrophe, and the introduction of an animal, almost as a *dramatis persona*, strain even the "surprise technique" of the Romances to the utmost. It may be recalled that the aged Goethe withdrew from the direction of the Weimar theatre because a dog was introduced upon the stage. It will be noticed, however, that the introduction of the *hunt* (not in Greene) at least provides a motive to explain both the bear and the presence of the shepherds on the shore.

**62. ancientry,** old people. The word suggested old people of grave and dignified bearing, and is used by Shakespeare elsewhere of this quality itself: "full of state and ancientry" (*Much Ado*, ii. 1. 80).

**67. browsing of ivy.** Greene, in the corresponding passage of the romance, is rather more specific. The shepherd goes to see whether his sheep are "browzing on the sea ivy, whereon they do feed".

**69. barne,** bairn, child. The word was obsolescent, except in northern and north-midland dialect, but is quoted by a clown in the proverbial phrase, "they say barnes are blessings" (*All's Well*, i. 3. 28), and serves Beatrice for a pun (*Much Ado*, iii. 4. 49).

a child. Probably the dialectal usage for a girl-child, exemplified by a writer in *Notes and Queries*, April 22, 1876 (quoted by Moorman, Arden edition), for Shropshire: "Is it a lad or a childe?"

**86. takes up,** overwhelms.

**90. yest,** yeast, foam. Not elsewhere in Shakespeare.

**94. flap-dragon'd,** swallowed.

**110. bearing-cloth,** the robe used to cover a child when taken to baptism.

**114. made;** Theobald's excellent emendation for Ff. *mad.*

**115. well to live,** "well to do".

**124. curst,** ill-tempered.

## Act IV—Scene 1

The dramatic awkwardness of a complete break in the story, not to be avoided if the story was to be dramatized at all, is unexampled in Shakespeare, and he has met it by an expedient almost equally without precedent in his drama. The action of *Henry V* was continuous, but it had long intervals, which he uses the Chorus to bridge. The nearest parallel is the Chorus to Act V, which has to explain "to those that have not read the story", how Henry and his army, in the interval since the end of Act IV, had returned from the field of Agincourt, enjoyed the triumphant welcome of London, and returned once more after a considerable interval (*v.* chorus 39–40) to France. The interval in the present case was less easy to deal with, but would certainly not have embarrassed Shakespeare's mature technique, had he chosen to apply it. A Chorus was a cheap and not unpopular short-cut, giving the requisite information without the need of inventing scene and dialogue. The present Chorus is correspondingly perfunctory in style, as Shakespeare is apt to be when, as in the finales of some of the comedies, he permits himself these "cheap short-cuts". The use of "Time" as the speaker was perhaps suggested by Greene's subtitle: "Pandosto, or the Triumph of Time".

**2. that makes and unfolds error.** The antecedent, Time, is irregularly thought of as the person described only, not as the person speaking. History is full of confusions and mis-understandings which "in time", as we say, are cleared up. "Time" is figuratively made responsible for both processes.

**8. one self-born hour,** a single hour of my own begetting. The expression is confused. All hours are thought of as Time's offspring; all are thence, for Time, "self-born"; the point here, however, is not this, but that in a *single* hour Time can "plant" and destroy a custom. The obscurity of the phrase was lessened for the Elizabethans by the survival of "self" in its original sense of "same" (e.g. "to shoot another arrow that *self* way which you did shoot the first", *Merchant of Venice*, i. 1. 148; &c.).

**9 f.** Time wishes simply to "pass" as of old, before there was any distinction of ancient or modern periods.

**24–5. now grown in grace Equal with wondering;** a not very pointed way of saying that her "grace" merited the wonder it excited.

**27–8. daughter . . . after.** The writer pronounced either *dafter* or *ater*; but it cannot be decided which, neither being Shakespearean, while both, as tested by rhyme or spelling, as shown by Moorman (Arden edition), were at least sporadic in the seventeenth century.

**29. allow,** approve.

## Scene 2

This short scene supplements the information provided by the Chorus. Its prose medium (both speakers have hitherto used verse) marks the transition from the tragic theme of Acts I–III to the homelier pastoral matter, breaking into exquisite lyric in the romance of Perdita and Florizel, which dominates in Acts IV–V, and for which the last lines of the scene prepare us.

5. **been aired abroad**, drawn breath, lived, abroad.

8. **allay**, abatement.

**o'erween**, am presumptuous enough.

19. **the heaping friendships**, the heaping up of friendly feelings. Polixenes will show his gratitude to Camillo still more emphatically than he has done already, looking for no reward but the closer knitting of the friendship between them.

23. **whose loss . . . are**; "are" is attracted to the plural by the intervening words, as often.

28. **approved**, proved.

31. **missingly noted**, i.e. noticed his absence.

34. Polixenes employs agents to watch Florizel in his seques-tered haunts.

46. **the angle**, the fishing rod with its hook. This figurative use survives in the verb, "to angle", while the noun is, as applied to fishing, obsolete.

## Scene 3

The scene gives us a pleasant first taste of Autolycus's quality. The duel of wits between him and the clown is a counterpart, in a more mischievous vein, of that between Touchstone and the Shepherd in *As You Like It*. But Touchstone establishes his superiority by dint of the veneer of court accomplishments which overlay his rustic breeding, Autolycus (though he has a touch of this veneer) by sheer native aptitude and want of scruple.

1 f, 15 f. Autolycus's song breathed, even more completely than he himself (for he has traits of the classical Mercury), the very atmosphere of the Elizabethan countryside, untouched by literary elegance or Arcadian sentiment. It may be compared with the lyrics in such literary Pastoral dramas as Fletcher's *Faithful Shepherdess* or Jonson's *Sad Shepherd*.

2. **doxy**, in thieves' slang, "sweetheart", "mistress". It still survives in dialect in this sense.

4. **the winter's pale**, the corporeal pallor of winter, contrasted with the ruddy freshness of spring. Literary tact vetoes the proposal to understand "pale" as "domain", "territory".

**7. pugging,** probably "thieving". The word is not exemplified, but "puggards" is used by Middleton as one of many words for, or varieties of, the thieving class.

**9. tirra-lirra,** a regular way of denoting the lark's song. So in French Moorman (ed.) quotes Du Bartas's *La Semaine*, "La gentille alouette avec son tire-lire".

**13. three-pile,** thick and costly velvet.

**20. budget,** wallet, pouch.

**24. Autolycus, &c.** In classical mythology Mercury had a son Autolycus, who inherited his cheating talent and propensity.

**26. die and drab,** dice and harlots.

**27. a silly cheat,** a fool. In thieves' slang of Shakespeare's time "cheat" stood for any person or thing, the special character of which was defined by the prefixed adjective. Cf. *New English Dictionary* under this word.

**28. Gallows and knock;** the application is explained by the next clause, the "knock" or "beating" referring to the disagreeable possibilities of the highwayman's career while in the exercise of his profession, the "gallows" to the incident which closed it if he was caught.

**31. tods,** yields a tod (28 lb.) of wool.

**41. three-man songmen,** singers of rounds or catches.

**42. means,** tenors.

**but one puritan, &c.** A puritan might be opposed to merrymaking, and so unsuitable to the purpose of the shearing-feast. But many puritans expressed their abhorrence of Rome by singing solemn words to vulgar or ludicrous music. The puritan in the present case is one of these.

**44. warden-pies,** pies of warden pears.

**45. out of my note,** outside my list of requisites for purchase. Even if the Clown was too illiterate to use a written list he carried a list in his head, which he figuratively calls his "note".

**47. raisins o' the sun,** grapes dried in the sun.

**50. I' the name of me!** "Me" has been supposed to be an incomplete word, such as "mercy"; but "me" is an unnatural abbreviation for this. If "me" is taken for the pronoun we may compare phrases like "body o' me".

**85. troll-my-dames,** the name of a game (Fr. *trou madame*) in which balls were trundled through arches set on a board (cf. Onions, *Shakespeare Glossary*).

**90. no more but abide.** The Clown clearly means merely make passing stay; but he is speaking as cleverly as he knows how, and his phrase is more pretentious than exact.

93. **compass'd a motion,** acquired a puppet-show. "Motion" was the regular term for such shows. Shakespeare plays on this sense in *Two Gentlemen of Verona*, ii. 1. 104. "The reference to the Prodigal Son is interesting as showing how biblical themes, once the subject of mystery plays, survived in the puppet-shows" (Moorman edition).

98. **prig,** a term for thief in thieves' slang, which had already obtained a wider currency, and has now, in a different sense, won a place in general colloquial English. As a verb it retains, of course, the original sense.

119. **unroll'd,** struck off the "roll" of beggars, i.e. removed from the register of his profession.

122. **hent,** lay hold of (and so get over).

## Scene 4

This "scene", one of the longest in Shakespeare, is dramatically a succession of scenes, in which different persons take part; the same place, the green-sward before the shepherd's cottage, being, in the literal sense of the word, the "scene" of all of them. The rapid and sudden changes of tone, import, and personnel, make this a good illustration of the technique of the later plays. The series of scenes may, for clearness, be distinguished somewhat as follows. After a prelude (Florizel and Perdita) we have (1) the festival, with the dialogue of Polixenes and Perdita (*v.* 55 *f.*). (2) Autolycus and the Clown and shepherd girls' homely comedy in contrast with the high poetry of (1) (*v.* 181 *f.*). (3) Polixenes's intervention; tragedy, or at least tragic "pity and terror", contrasted with the previous idyll (*v.* 336 *f.*). (4) Camillo's plot with Florizel (*v.* 455 *f.*). (5) Autolycus makes game of the Shepherd (*v.* 662 *f.*).

3. **Peering in April's front,** i.e. at the beginning of April. So, "Philomel in summer's front doth sing" (*Sonnet* 102). Greene had already compared his heroine in her festal garb to Flora; Shakespeare lifts the conventional comparison into poetry by this exquisite touch.

8. **mark o' the land.** Florizel is "the observed of all observers", as another royal prince, Hamlet, is called by another secretly worshipping maiden, Ophelia.

12. **with a custom,** from habit.

13. **swoon,** Hanmer's emendation for Folio *sworn*, which makes neither grammar nor sense. To object, as has been done, that Perdita is not the person to swoon, is to mistake the figurative character of such asseverations. She is merely expressing in a lively way her native disinclination to such "follies".

14. **To show myself in a glass**, i.e. if she saw herself in one.

**I bless the time, &c.** In this single vivid sentence Shakespeare conveys all that is important in Greene's account of the hawking expedition in which "Dorestus" first saw "Fawnia".

17. **difference**, i.e. of rank.

33. **in a way so chaste**, with so chaste an aim.

40. **Or I my life.** Perdita means that unless Florizel gives up his project her life will be forfeited. The two "necessities" are alternatives, one of which will be realized, but not both. Furness's explanation (adopted in Arden edition) that she means "change my *way* of life", i.e. cease to "queen it" and become a simple shepherdess once more, is therefore wrong, since this would be a consequence, not the alternative, of Florizel's giving up his claim to her hand.

55 f. This is one of the most delightful of Shakespeare's descriptive portraits of persons not in the drama. Other famous ones are the Bastard's of the Traveller (*King John*, i. 1. 189 *f.*) and Hotspur's of the Courtier on the battle-field (*1 Henry IV*, i. 3. 30 *f.*).

56. **pantler**, a pantry attendant.

64. **bid . . . to 's welcome**, bid them welcome to us.

75. **Seeming**, seemliness, comeliness.

76. **Grace and remembrance, &c.** They were symbolized by the flowers which she has just offered them, rue and rosemary respectively. So Ophelia (*Hamlet*, iv. 5. 180). *Remembrance*, as four syllables; the groups *br*, *tr*, occasionally having syllabic value in Shakespeare. So "that croaks the fatal entrance of Duncan" (*Macbeth*, i. 5. 40).

82. **gillyvors** (a naturalized form of Middle English *gilofre*, further accommodated to English speech instinct in the current "gillyflower").

83. **nature's bastards;** she means, as her following words show, that the gillyvors are not a spontaneous natural growth, but have been artificially crossed, the "streaks" being the result of the crossing.

85. **Wherefore, gentle maiden, &c.** Polixenes's question and his ensuing dialogue with Perdita, though among the most beautiful and famous passages in Shakespeare, would be dramatically irrelevant, and therefore un-Shakespearean, but for the ironical reference, of which both are unconscious, to the affair which has brought them together, where their parts in the present colloquy are soon to be reversed. "Before the scene is over, we witness the ungovernable fury of Polixenes

that the 'gentler scion' that has sprung from his own loins should marry the 'wildest stock' that has grown up in the home of the shepherd" (Moorman).

89. mean, means, agency.

90. nature makes that mean. The "artificial" process of grafting itself depends for success upon the living power of nature.

112. my fair'st friend; she turns to Florizel, and the whole of her following speech, woven of the most entrancing flower-poetry, is redolent of her maiden passion. This is the clue to the sometimes daring beauty of the epithets.

116. Proserpina, according to the legend (well known to Shakespeare from Ovid's *Metamorphoses*), was seized by Pluto (Dis) as she was gathering flowers at Enna in Sicily, and carried away to become queen of the underworld. Cf. Milton's equally beautiful allusion (*Paradise Lost*, iv. 268 *f.*), a good opportunity for a comparison between Shakespeare's and Milton's way of handling briefly the same story, and between Shakespearean and Miltonic blank verse; for though Shakespeare's blank verse has almost countless varieties, Milton's is unlike them all.

119. take, charm, captivate as by magic.

120. dim; referring to the violet's dark unobtrusive hue, in implicit contrast with the radiant splendour of Juno and Venus, whom the violet nevertheless surpasses by its fragrance.

126. The crown imperial, the tall, yellow fritillary (*Fritillaria imperialis*) (Moorman).

132. quick, alive. She breaks off suddenly, conscious of the daring frankness into which her ardour has betrayed her, and excuses it as "acting".

134. Whitsun pastorals, the morris-dances in character, Robin Hood and Maid Marian being usually the persons played, which were customary in the countryside at Whit-suntide.

143. each your doing . . . Crowns what you are doing, &c. This is merely a not very lucid expansion of his opening phrase (135-6). Every act of Perdita has a unique charm of its own, and thus stands supreme among all actions of the same kind.

148. The verse cannot have been written by Shakespeare as it stands, but no plausible emendation has been suggested. Capell's "so fairly" and Staunton's "which though it fairly peeps" are equally intolerable.

152. skill, reason.

157. nothing she does or seems, &c. Shakespeare is a

firm believer in the manifestation, by indelible symptoms, of royal race; a belief which he shared with the folk tales, and doubtless derived from them.

**160. look out**, Theobald's excellent emendation for Ff. *look on't*. The figure is that of *v.* 148, but the shade of meaning different; Perdita referring to the natural ruddiness of a healthy body, Camillo to the heightened crimson of a blush.

**169. feeding**, pasturage.

**176. featly**, gracefully.

**194. dildos and fadings**, meaningless burdens found in various old ballads.

**197. admirable conceited**, marvellously ingenious.

**198. unbraided**, new, not spoiled or worn (*braided*) by use.

**200. points**; a play on the two senses (1) tagged laces, (2) "points" in an argument.

**202. inkles**, tapes; **caddises**, worsted laces.

**204. sleeve-hand**, wrist-band, cuff.

**205. square**, the part of the dress which covered the breast, usually adorned with embroidery.

**214. cypress**, crape.

**217. Bugle**, of black beads.

**221. poking-sticks**, rods used for stiffening the plaits of ruffs. They were first heated in the fire. Hence the advice given in Middleton's *Blurt Master Constable*: "Your ruff must stand in print, and for that purpose get poking-sticks with fair long handles, lest they scorch your hands".

**237. plackets**, stomachers.

**239. kiln-hole**, the fire-place used in making malt; said to be, like the ingle-nook, a favourite place for confidential gossip.

**241. clamour**, restrain, stop. A rare survival of M.E. *clameren* (O.N. *klambra*), press, clasp close; hence, of the tongue, silence (Gollancz). So Taylor the water-poet: "*Clamour* the proclamation of your tongues."

**243. tawdry-lace**, a silken neckerchief, originally sold at the Fair of St. Etheldreda (Awdrey) at Ely, of whose cathedral she was the patron saint.

**251. charge**, value.

**253. a life**, on my life.

**258. carbonadoed**, slashed, cut in slices.

**292. Whither . . . thither.** The Ff. forms, *whether . . . thether*, which were widely current in colloquial Elizabethan, were probably in the original song, as suggested by the rhyme *neither*.

303. **sad**, serious.

316. **utter**, offer for sale.

319. **men of hair**, dressed in skins, like satyrs.

   **Saltiers**, for "satyrs".

320. **gallimaufry**, mixture, hotch-potch.  Cf. Pistol's use of the word in *Merry Wives*, ii. 1. 119.

323. **some that know little but bowling**, i.e. courtly persons; bowling being then an aristocratic game.

328. With this speech of Polixenes compare the similar reply of Theseus to the suggestion that such "homely foolery" is not for him (*Midsummer-Night's Dream*, v. 1, 81 *f.*).

332. **squier**, foot-rule.

336. **O father**, &c.  During the dance Polixenes has been in conversation with the old Shepherd.  At the close of the dance he breaks off the talk with these words.  To the import of the talk there is no clue.

341. **handed**, handled, engaged in.

342. **my she**.  Both *she* and *he* occur constantly as substantives.  So "any he", &c.

   **knacks**, trinkets.

345. **marted with**, purchased of.

346 f. put a wrong construction on it.

347. **straited**, put to straits, hard pressed.

351. **looks**, looks for.

357. **bolted**, sifted.

362 f. With this speech of Florizel and Polixenes's comment, compare those of Ferdinand and Prospero in a similar situation (*Tempest*, iv. 1. 23).

374. **nor mean better**, &c.  Florizel has expressed an ideal of married life as high as her own, and though she cannot put it into words, she uses her own pure intentions to interpret his.  The image is, of course, a "feminine" one, from dressmaking.  Cf. Imogen's, in a more tragic situation (*Cymbeline*, iii. 4. 33).  The numerous cases of analogous phrases, speeches, and situations, in the latest group of plays, should be noted and collected by the student.

393. **dispute his own estate**, discuss his own property, affairs.

399. **reason**, it is reasonable that; a common elliptical construction.

413. **affects**, for *affectst*.  So, after simple -t, "thou ... revisits thus the glimpses of the moon" (*Hamlet*, i. 4. 53).

415. **piece**, paragon.  The word was idiomatically applied

to anything excellent, or supreme, of its kind, especially to persons; e.g. " Thy mother was a piece of virtue " (*Tempest*, i. 2. 56).

**421. knack**; cf. *v.* 342. Polixenes uses the same word, but now contemptuously.

**424. Farre**, further. This is the comparative, still surviving in Elizabethan, of M.E. *fer* (*far*). The form *ferre* is also found, but *e*, as in all cases where *-er* was followed by a consonant, was in the sixteenth century already pronounced *a*.

**428. him too,** &c. Florizel may be " worthy enough " of Perdita too, since his behaviour puts him below her, and the " worth " which sets him immeasurably above her is derived solely from his royal blood.

**439. alike**, indifferently.

**448. the bed my father died.** A parallel construction to (e.g.) " the day my father died ", " where " being understood, as there " when ".

**464. I not purpose it.** Word-order was in many respects freer in Elizabethan English. The negative " not ", now used (1) before the verb (in categorical sentences) only in combina- tion with an auxiliary (" do not ", &c.), and (2) after it, rarely except in verse, could still be used, as here and in about a score of other places in Shakespeare, all in blank verse, without auxiliary before it. E.g. " I not doubt " (*Tempest*, ii. 1. 121); " whereof the ewe not bites " (v. 1. 38), &c. But it was already becoming unusual. Cowper's " cup that cheers but not inebri- ates ", nearly two hundred years later, was definitely archaic, even in verse. Our " do not ", " cannot ", " have not ", &c., are survivals of (2) in current prose, the negative having coalesced with the preceding verb. But in America " have not " is felt to be " poetical " (like " go not ", &c.), and is replaced by " do not (don't) have ".

**475. fancy**, love.

**496. benefit your knowledge**, profit you if you knew it.

**504. Purchase**, procure.

**507. curious**, anxious, exacting.

**518. ponderous**, weighty.

**525. with my best endeavours,** &c. There is probably an anacoluthon, or unconscious change of construction; the subject of " strive " being Camillo, not Florizel. The absent Florizel can do nothing to " qualify " his father's anger; this is to be the work of Camillo, who will use his " best endeavours " for that end.

**542. free**, willing.

**545. o'er and o'er divides him,** i.e. between the thought of his former cruelty to the father and his new-found love for the son.

**571. take in**, get into its power, overcome.

**Yea, say you so?** &c. The old counsellor is astonished at such a reply from a simple shepherd girl.

**575. i' the rear o' her birth**, i.e. behind in respect of birth, low-born. This is a necessary correction of Folio *our*, which destroys the balance of the thought. Florizel is not comparing Perdita with himself either in birth or breeding, but saying that she has the quality of the high-bred with the status of the low-born.

**581. medicine**, physician. This meaning, though not necessary (since the figurative sense could stand) is probable. Cf. "Meet we the medicine of the sickly weal, And with him pour we in our country's purge Each drop of us" (*Macbeth*, v. 2. 27).

**583. appear**, be regarded as such.

**592. pomander**, ball of perfumes.

**table-book**, memorandum book.

**597. best in picture**, most attractive to the eye (of the pickpocket), i.e. bulkiest.

**600. pettitoes**, a jocular term for feet (properly, pig's feet).

**608. whoo-bub**, an older form of "hubbub"; not elsewhere in Shakespeare.

**616. Who.** The interrogative and relative "who" is often in Elizabethan English used for *whom*; as a relative, with an antecedent governed by a verb, *whom* is constantly used (by attraction) for *who*.

**629. boot**, compensation. In money value Autolycus would anyhow have the best of the bargain, his "garments" being inferior to Florizel's; Camillo, however, adds a present, to lubricate his movements. As compensation for the "compulsory" exchange, this may still be properly called "boot".

**637. earnest**, i.e. a first instalment, viz. Camillo's present. Cf. Autolycus's reflections on the transaction, *v.* 662 *f.* below.

**640. prophecy**, i.e. in calling her "fortunate".

**646. over**, i.e. on you. The expression is awkward, and the text not free from doubt. Rowe read *over you*. Schmidt's "For I do fear eyes—over to shipboard" gives a bad rhythm.

**671. clog**, encumbrance.

**699. fardel**, bundle.

**705. excrement**, i.e. his (false) beard. The word has in Shakespeare almost always its literal meaning of a "growth", especially of the human hair or beard. Cf. "Why is Time such a niggard of hair, being as it is so plentiful an excrement?" (*Comedy of Errors*, ii. 2. 79).

708. **condition**, nature.

710. **having**, property.

716. **they do not give us the lie**, i.e. they *sell* it, since "we pay them for it".

719. **taken yourself with the manner**, taken yourself in the act, i.e. of being "given the lie", as Autolycus had just declared "us soldiers" often to be. To be "taken with the manner" (O.F. *manoeavre*, L. *manu*) was a law phrase used of a criminal taken "red-handed", or in the very act.

721 f. Autolycus's quick wit at once sees the superior opportunities of the "courtier" rôle, suggested by the Shepherd's simple question, and instantly changes over into the appropriate style and vocabulary. Compare Falstaff's parody of the courtly style (*1 Henry IV*, ii. 4. 440).

726. **toaze**, touse, tear.

741. **His garments are rich.** This is probably an oversight, Florizel's dress, which Autolycus is wearing, having been "a swain's wearing" (*v.* 9 above), not his customary garb as a prince. No doubt it would be the swain's "Sunday best", matching the festal dress of Perdita; but that is not enough to account for the Shepherd's remark.

745. **picking on's teeth**, a fashionable habit. Cf. Falconbridge's sketch of the "traveller" at his future table (*King John*, i. 1. 190).

760. **in hand-fast**, in custody.

765. **germane**, akin; a learned term (cf. note to 721 *f.*).

775. **He has a son, who**, &c. The following description follows with little variation that which Shakespeare had read in Boccaccio's story of Ambrogiuolo (*Decameron*, ii. 9), the immediate source of the wager story in *Cymbeline*. Ambrogiuolo is the original of Iachimo, and expiates his crime by the death decribed, instead of receiving the "mercy" magnanimously awarded (in the large spirit of the later Shakespeare) by Posthumus.

780. **prognostication**, i.e. in one of the published almanacs.

786. **being something gently consider'd**, if I receive a fair "consideration".

805. **case**; a play on the two senses.

## Act V—Scene 1

The action returns to the Sicilian court. Little attempt is made to provide evidence of the passage there of the sixteen years requisitioned by the dramatist to enable Perdita to grow up in Bohemia. Leontes reappears, indistinguishable from the penitent king who had retired at the close of Act iii, Scene 2. Paulina is her old self, sleepless champion of his slandered wife, and not a whit mellowed by the years of his "saint-like sorrow". But the court has begun to hint discreetly at the need of an heir, and therefore of a second marriage. Paulina meets this with brilliant diplomatic skill, first pointing to the oracle's declaration that Leontes would not have an heir, and then guiding him tactfully, step by step, into the trap which is also to be the solution of the whole trouble—his consent to take, should he marry, only a wife whom she would provide. The climax of the Hermione-Leontes story appears to be in sight. But the situation thus successfully arranged is disturbed, within the limits of the present scene, by two events, equally startling to the persons on the stage, and of romantically contrasted import,—the arrival of Florizel and Perdita, unattended, and the reported arrival of Polixenes and Camillo. With his usual delicate instinct Shakespeare transforms a repulsive trait in Greene's narrative at this point into an added beauty. Greene had made the king openly and persistently court his unknown daughter; Leontes feels the charm of her beauty, and his admiring gaze alarms for a moment the ever suspicious Paulina. But his words to Florizel are a playful jest, and his reply to Paulina, " I thought of [Hermione] even in those looks I made", hints at incipient recognition that it is Hermione's daughter that stands before him.

19. **good now**, a persuasive mode of address, often accompanying a merely courteous request, as in "good now, sit down and tell me, he that knows" (Marcellus to Horatio and his friends after the first appearance of the Ghost, *Hamlet*, i. 1. 70); often entreating, as here.

27. **fail**, failure.

29. **Incertain**, irresolute.

35. **Respecting**, in respect of, in comparison with.

52. **squared**, fitted, adjusted.

59. (**Where we offenders now**). The Folios have "(where we offenders now appeare)", leaving the principal sentence without a verb. If the reading is otherwise genuine, "appeare" was probably by oversight understood as the predicate of both sentences. Otherwise the bracketed words in the text must be regarded as a harshly compressed construction. "Move" for "now" is a plausible conjecture.

50. **Why to me?** i.e. why this humiliation?

66. **rift**, split.

75. **Affront**, confront.

84. **Enter a Gentleman.** Folios, *a Servant.* Theobald's substitution of "a Gentleman" is justified by his following speeches. Cf. especially *v.* 98, 102.

90. **out of circumstance**, unceremoniously.

108. **professors**, adherents of the faith "professed" by the sect.

113. **assisted with**, attended by; cf. "the king and prince at prayers! let us assist them!" (*The Tempest*, i. 1. 57).

137. **my life**, an adverbial phrase, during my life.

140. **at friend**, in friendship.

142. **worn times**, old age.

149. **offices**, attentions, especially as here those expressed in courteous words.

170. **climate**, sojourn under our skies. "Climate" was properly a region of the heaven, hence used of the region of the earth under it.

171. **graceful**, gracious.

182. **attach**, arrest.

187. **amazedly**, confusedly.

198. **in question**, under examination.

230. **Your honour, &c.**, i.e. provided that your honour be not, &c.

## Scene 2

It has excited surprise that one of the great dramatic moments of the plot, the union and recognition of Leontes and his child (together with Paulina's first intelligence of her husband's fate) should not be represented but told, and that in narrative prose of the most affected and mannered type. Precisely the most pathetic moments are, in fact, conveyed in phrases most calculated to banish pathos (cf. *v.* 71 *f.*, of Paulina, with the similar phraseology of the King's diplomatic oration in *Hamlet*, i. 2. 11, "With an auspicious and a dropping eye"). The probable explanation, first suggested by Harness, is that Shakespeare deliberately kept this first "recognition" low and flat in tone in order to give its full emotional and dramatic value to the true climax of the play, the great recognition scene which closes it.

11. **were very notes of admiration**, expressions of utter astonishment. "Note", a sign by which anything is known, hence, of a passion or other mental quality, its expression in

the face, as in "a note infallible of breaking honesty" (above
i. 2. 270).

12. **cases of their eyes,** eyelids.

18. **importance,** import.

30. **pregnant by circumstance,** made convincing by circum-
stantial evidence (such as the speaker gives in the remainder
of his speech). Similarly the adverb, e.g.:

> "A thousand moral paintings I can show
> That shall demonstrate these quick blows of Fortune
> More frequently than words."

36. **affection,** disposition.

46. **countenance,** demeanour. So "puts my apparel and my
countenance on" (*Taming of the Shrew*, i. 1. 234).

48. **favour,** features.

54. **weather-bitten,** corroded by the weather.

57. **to do it,** to express it. *Do* was used specifically of
artistic or literary expression, hence could be equivalent to
write, paint, carve, or build. Cf. 94, and 98 below, "he so
near to Hermione hath done Hermione".

60. **Like an old tale still;** Shakespeare again (as in the
title and elsewhere) turns the point of rationalist criticism of
his plot by emphasizing its *Märchen* character.

95. **Julio Romano** (Giulio R.), a famous painter and sculptor
of the Italian Renascence. That he is introduced as a contemporary of the oracle of Delphi is no anomaly in the technique
of the "Romances". What Shakespeare knew of him and his
work cannot now be determined. Several of his pictures were
in Whitehall in the time of Charles I, and may, as Elze pointed
out, have been in the small collection originally formed by
Henry VIII. But whether Shakespeare had seen any of his
work or not, it would be strange if, in 1610, a man who had
lived for a dozen years in intimacy with the literary world, and
in not remote touch with the court, had not acquired as much
knowledge or half-knowledge about a famous Italian artist as
he shows here. It is clear, moreover, that he thought of the
statue as *coloured* like life.

105. **piece,** piece out, increase.

109. **unthrifty to our knowledge,** neglectful of the chance
of increasing it.

120. **relish'd,** had a pleasant or gratifying flavour (as a discovery might be expected to have), hence, found acceptance.

144. **preposterous;** he means prosperous; but the blunder
has unconscious irony as suggesting the absurd inversion of
his real and his apparent status.

157. **franklins,** yeomen.

161. **tall,** vigorous, bold. It was used especially of muscular vigour with arms and hands (in fighting or otherwise). Hence the phrases "a tall man (or fellow) of thy (his) hands". Cf. *v.* 164.

## Scene 3

This great and beautiful scene is unlike any other in Shakespeare. It effects the reunions and recognitions which normally closed the "Romance" comedies, but in a way, so far as we know, entirely original. Shakespeare, so sensitive to music and its power, shows little interest in painting and less in sculpture; and his use of the (imaginary) statue here, as of the pictures in *Hamlet*, betrays no conception that art can have any value beyond that of giving a faithful "likeness". It will be noticed that when Hermione is at length recognized, it is her reunion with Perdita, not with Leontes, upon which the whole emotional stress is laid. She embraces him, but does not once address him, and he only once, at the close, addresses her. Of the lofty forgiveness pronounced by Posthumus upon Iachimo (*Cymbeline,* v. 5. 418), as of his agonized remorse for the wrong he has done his wife (*ibid.* 226 *f.*), and rapturous reunion with her (*ibid.* 263 *f.*), there is equally little question here. On the other hand, the reunion of mother and daughter touches a chord of emotion all but unexampled elsewhere in Shakespeare. Most of his heroines have no mothers; and his mothers (Elizabeth, Constance, even Gertrude) lavish passion and solicitude only on their sons.

52. The metrical incompleteness of the line is perhaps not authentic; but its diction is flawless, and none of the suggested emendations (such as "nor ever sorrow") fits perfectly into its place.

56. **Polixenes** wishes that he could relieve Leontes's grief by enhancing (*piecing*) his own till it reaches the same measure. "Up" emphasizes the statement (conveyed by "so much . . . as") that this measure is reached.

67. **fixure,** fixity. Her eye is represented with such veracity that it seems capable of motion, like a living eye.

68. **As we are mock'd with art,** for so we . . . ; not "as if we are (were) mocked", as interpreted by Malone and others. For Leontes believes that he is looking at a real work of art, and that he is really "mocked" by its life-like character, as he might be by any other work of similar realism.

86. **presently,** immediately.

96. **On.** This is Paulina's summons to those who are waiting her signal for the decisive movement. She breaks off to bid any disaffected spectators to withdraw. Then Leontes supports

her with his "Proceed", and she resumes with the explicit command: "Music, &c."

100. **all that look upon**, all onlookers. "To look upon" is regularly "to be a spectator". So (of Richard II surrounded by his captors): "all of you that stand and look upon" (*Richard II*, iv. 1. 237).

107. **double**, twice.

117. **Like an old tale**; cf. note v. 2. 60.

129. **upon this push**, under the impulse of this occasion.

132. **Partake to**, share with.

144. **whose**, probably Paulina's, not Camillo's.

147. **What! &c.** Leontes turns for the first (and only) time to address Hermione. The construction of the following sentence (*v.* 149 *f.*) is perplexed, "whom", the subject of "is troth-plight", being governed by "directing"—"who, by heavens' direction".

# APPENDIX

## PROSODY

### SUMMARY

## I. VERSE AND PROSE

1. Quite contrary to classical[1] and other foreign precedent, Shakespeare, like most of his contemporaries and successors, mingled verse and prose in the same play, in the same scene, and even in the same speech.

2. Up to about 1597 the distribution between them which prevails later in his work is not yet established. The influence of Marlowe in particular made for the uniform use of verse; this is almost exclusively used in the early Histories, while in the later (*1* and *2 Henry IV* and *Henry V*) about half is prose. It may be taken as certain that had *King John* (e.g.) been written in 1599 the earlier speeches of Falconbridge would have been prose. From about 1597 onwards the distribution is

---

[1] The use of different metres for scenes of different emotional quality (especially *senarii* and *tetrameters*) in Greek tragedy and in comedy made a certain approach to this in principle, as did the far more extensive use of varied metres in the contemporary (but unknown) Spanish drama.

guided by certain principles, which can in general be recognized. The precise explanation of particular passages is often doubtful. But it is important to realize that the use of prose and verse is never arbitrary.

3. These principles may be stated thus: *Verse* is used, normally, (*a*) to emphasize *passion*, in situation or in character. It accompanies a heightened emotional temperature, and often marks the sudden passage of a scene into this heightened mood. Thus, when the funeral procession, headed by the king and queen, approaches the graveyard at Elsinore, Hamlet and Horatio break off their prose colloquy upon the dust of Alexander with:

> But soft! but soft! aside: here comes the king.
>
> (*Hamlet*, v. 1. 240.)

So, without any such outer provocation, Volumnia's exultation in her son suddenly breaks through the sober vesture of prose into lyric:

These are the ushers of Marcius: before him he carries noise, and behind him he leaves tears:

> Death, that dark spirit, in 's nervy arm doth lie,
> Which, being advanced, declines, and then men die.
>
> (*Coriolanus*, ii. 1. 171 *f.*)

(*b*) Though this principle is less consistently applied, verse is recognized as *nobler*, and therefore more appropriate to high-born persons; and as these, in Shakespeare, habitually play the leading part in the action, the framework of the plot, and the crucial scenes, are normally in verse. Verse may hence also mark the ceremonial or deferential language of subordinate or low-class characters. It may also be the medium of quite prosaic and matter-of-fact statements by noble persons, e.g. the archbishop's justification of the king's title (*Henry V*, i. 2. 32 *f.*), one of the flattest passages in Shakespeare.

Naturally these "principles" are not consistent, and frequently interfere with one another in practice. The one reflects the sensitive literary instinct of Shakespeare the poet, the other the aristocratic prejudices of Shakespeare the man.

4. In the absence of either of these motives for verse, prose is normal. Clearly this may arise from several distinct causes. Thus prose is the normal medium of (*a*) *low-class* characters: the *plebeians* at Rome (*Julius Cæsar, Coriolanus*); sailors (*Tempest, Hamlet*); Trinculo and Stephano (*Tempest*); the players and gravediggers (*Hamlet*); while in the immature Histories the citizens (*Richard III*) and the gardeners (*Richard II*) speak blank verse.

But when low-class characters have passion and pathos, like the murderers in *Macbeth*, they use verse. And note that Caliban, though treated as a slave by Prospero, speaks only in *verse*, a significant hint that this scion of the unspoilt new world is after all regarded as less ignoble than the dregs of civilization with whom he conspires.

(*b*) *Comic* situations and characters. This often concurs with (*a*) as in the porter (*Macbeth*), the gravediggers (*Hamlet*), Dogberry and Verges, and most of the *clowns* and *jesters*. But Falstaff, though well-born, also speaks exclusively prose, except when he is parodying the "noble" manner of the stage-court (*1 Henry IV*, 4. 431).

(*c*) Sardonic, cynical, sarcastic characters, moods, and situations: e.g. Don John (*Much Ado*), Lucio (*Measure for Measure*), and the patrician Menenius (*Coriolanus*); so most of the bitter colloquies of Hamlet; while in his soliloquies bitterness is lifted into passion.

(*d*) Matter-of-fact, drily "realistic", "prosaic" characters, moods, situations.

Thus documents and letters, when quoted; e.g. Macbeth's (*Macbeth*, i. 5), Posthumus's (*Cymbeline*, iii. 2, iv. 4).

(*e*) Distinct from these is the use of prose for the incoherent language of *madness* (Lear, Edgar, Ophelia), frenzy, or mental paralysis.

5. But these various motives for prose or verse rarely occur singly. They are therefore often in conflict, and the decision in favour of one or the other is a means of delicate dramatic effects. Thus the most romantic and noble persons habitually speak prose with the Clown; and Falstaff's powerful magnetism creates prose wherever he moves. Hamlet speaks prose not only when he is sarcastic, but in his first cordial welcome to, or, later, in earnest expostulation with, the insignificant Rosencrantz and Guildenstern.

We may now apply these general laws of Shakespeare's prose and verse to the present play. Like so much else in the later Plays, when compared with the tragedies or even with the middle comedies, the distinction between prose and verse is carried out on simple lines, and requires little discussion.

Taking the characters separately we find that *Leontes, Hermione, Paulina, Florizel,* and *Perdita,* the principal personages of the serious story, and all of those courtly or noble birth (known or otherwise), speak uniformly, and *Polixenes* and *Camillo* normally, *blank verse,* 3 (*b*).

The old *Shepherd,* who usually speaks prose, in the festive exaltation of a great occasion, when "unknown friends", evidently of distinction, are present, speaks verse (iv. 4), 3 (*b*).

The *Gaoler,* similarly (ii. 2), in addressing Paulina, speaks verse; his sympathy, notwithstanding his office, with his prisoner and her advocate being thus unobtrusively marked.

*Autolycus,* on the contrary, the *Shepherd* (apart from the above case), the *Clown,* the *Servant* (iv. 4), *Mopsa,* and *Dorcas* speak habitually prose, 4 (*a*). In iv. 4. 161 *f.,* the Clown and the farm girls speak a few lines of verse. But here, like the old Shepherd, as the Clown says, they are "standing upon their manners". It is equally according to rule that the official charge against Hermione, and the oracle, both documents read in court, are in prose, 4 (*d*). In a few scenes prose is assigned to noble or courtly persons for special purposes. Thus scene i. 1., between Archidamus and Camillo, is a merely preliminary, matter of fact colloquy, the pedestrian form of which gives emphasis to the *pathos* of the scene which succeeds.

A similar explanation applies to the prose colloquy of *Polixenes* and *Camillo* (v. 2) which ushers in the glowing poetry of the idyll.

The prose description by "Gentlemen" of so passionate a scene as the restoration of Perdita to her father (v. 2) may seem anomalous. But the narrations (mostly not by an eye-witness) is deliberately matter of fact (see note to the scene); it is also addressed to *Autolycus*.

We may note how Camillo, in the space of a few lines, speaks verse to Florizel, prose to Autolycus, and then verse to Perdita (whose inborn nobility he recognizes, but whose actual birth he does not yet know) (iv. 4. 612–648).


## II. RHYME

Save occasionally, to mark the close of a scene, when it occurs in the final couplet, rhyme was no longer used at this date in *dialogue*.

Apart from the *songs*, it occurs only in the extra-dramatic address of *Time* (iv. 1).


## III. SCANSION

### 1. Elizabethan Pronunciation

1. The current pronunciation of English in Elizabethan times differed widely from ours, and some of the differences affect the proper scansion of their verse.

Thus (i) the accent sometimes fell on a different syllable: e.g. *contráct* (noun):

> Mark our contract.—Mark your divorce, young sir (iv. 4. 410).

*Médicinal*

> Do come with words as medicinal as true (ii. 3. 37).

(ii) Syllables now pronounced were *slurred*:

> As you are certainly a *gentleman*, thereto (two syllables) (i. 2. 375).

but

> When I shall see this *gentleman*, thy speeches (three syllables) (v. 1. 121).

Conversely, syllables now slurred were pronounced. The most important example of this kind is the ending -*tion*, -*sion*, still in sixteenth century verse often of two syllables. But its pronunciation and scansion as one syllable was rapidly growing. In *The Winter's Tale* both are found: e.g. (two syllables):

> Yet, for a greater confirmation (ii. 1. 172).

So iii. 1. 15; iii. 2. 7 (one syllable):

> To have her honour true than your suspicion (ii. 1. 152).

The student should collect the examples of both scansions. So in other cases; as *business* (three syllables) (iv. 4. 406). But *business* (two syllables) (i. 2. 214).

## 2. METRE: GENERAL CHARACTERISTICS

1. The *norm* of English blank verse is a line of five metrical beats, separated in pronunciation by equal intervals of time.

The simplest representation of the norm is a verse in which the five beats fall upon five naturally-stressed syllables, the interval preceding each being filled by five syllables without stress.

Such verses occur occasionally in *The Winter's Tale*; e.g.

> That cóme befóre the swállow dáres, and táke (iv. 4. 119).

But the sequence of five metrical beats can be satisfied in many other ways, just as in music an infinity of tunes comply with a given rhythmic basis. And in verse, too, the beauty lies in the new groupings of sound discovered by the melodic instinct of the poet. Almost everything that enters into verse—number of syllables, number of stresses, degree of stress—is variable, provided that the sense of metrical sequence is maintained. Thus a verse can have a stress on every syllable, or on no more than four, or even three, as in Shelley's

> Undulate with the úndulating tíde.

And it can have more than one unstressed syllable, not only, as here, between the stresses, but between the metrical beats.

2. But further, in the verse of Elizabethan drama, including Shakespeare, not only are the musical varieties played on the norm inexhaustible; the norm itself is often relaxed or suspended; in other words, an approach is made to the freedom of conversation; a natural, though not necessary (and in other schools of drama very unusual), characteristic of dramatic dialogue. Thus Shakespeare constantly admits verses both shorter and longer than the norm, and quite incapable of being reduced to it. It is certain that both dramatic realism and joy in the endless wealth of his musical invention had their part in determining the form and character of his verse. But the

attempt to discriminate between the two formative influences is for the most part impracticable, and, in any case, cannot be attempted here.

In *The Winter's Tale* the verse, unlike the diction, offers little that is irregular or abnormal. In pure beauty of rhythm its finest passages (as in the first part of Act iv. 4) are surpassed by nothing that Shakespeare has written. And this excellence is won not by the use of strange or daring metrical effects, but by a consummate mastery of the actual though hitherto rarely explored musical resources of the metre. One of these resources Shakespeare does now indeed use with a freedom which even in the days of the great tragedies he had not permitted himself. But this—the "light ending"—now becomes the instrument precisely of his most beautiful rhythmical effects; being felt, not as an interruption of the melody of the single line, but as a link in a larger and richer metrical movement—a verse paragraph.

### 3. Normal Variations

#### (i) *Extra Syllables*

The normal "decasyllabic" verse was never, in English, strictly limited to ten syllables. At the outset, in Chaucer, the unstressed extra syllable at the end ("feminine ending") even predominated, as it did in Italian, where the verse was thence more accurately called "eleven-syllabled" (*endecasillabo*). And beside that, Chaucer could put two unstressed syllables for one, and even drop the unstressed syllable of the first foot, producing verses of nine, and even twelve, syllables, as well as eleven and ten. In other words, the native tradition of a constant number of stresses survives in him along with the French tradition of a constant number of syllables; and each tradition supplements and modifies the other.

The first blank verse was severely decasyllabic, as in Surrey's *Æneid* and in *Gorboduc*. A great advance towards variety of verse music was made, when this rigour came to be relaxed, in two ways, (1) by the recovery of the Chaucerian unstressed final (eleventh) syllable, (2) by the reassertion of the native (and also classical) tradition of *equivalence*.

In its simplest form this appears in the substitution of a foot (x x —') for (x —'): this is common everywhere in Shakespeare, but, like all other forms of metrical emancipation, gains ground as he advances.

It is found (1) within a word or clause. In the present play this occurs almost exclusively where the extra syllable is slight (usually formed by a liquid and a vowel). This is one source of its even music:

> Thy by-gone *fooleries* were but spices of it (iii. 2. 180).
> *Hermione* was not so much wrinkled, nothing (v. 3. 28).

(2) Before, or after, a strong pause, especially at the close of a speech:

> This is put forth too truly: besides, I have stay'd (i. 2. 14).

Even *two extra unstressed syllables* may thus be introduced. While the single unstressed final syllable (*feminine ending*) is found in all periods of Shakespeare's work, in all his later verse, his hypermetrical unstressed syllables are admitted, not only at the end, but within the line, usually before a pause (1) at the end:

> And leave you to your graver steps.  Hermione (i. 2. 173).

(2) Within the line:

> Were there necess | ity | in your request, although (i. 2. 22).
> Of head-piece extraord | inar | y? lower messes (i. 2. 213).

### (ii) *Variation in the Pauses*

Language, in verse, is a succession of sounds which arrange themselves spontaneously for us in two distinct series of groups:

1. *Sense* groups—clauses, sentences.
2. *Metrical* groups—feet, verses.

The earliest English blank verse tended to make these groups coincide, and this tendency is still very perceptible in the early verse of Shakespeare, as in that of Marlowe.

But as he advances he tends more and more to make the groups not concide but overlap.  A growing proportion of sentences, and a smaller, but also growing, proportion of clauses, ends within the verse, not at its close.  An important case of the first is the speech-endings, which also, it is found, increasingly occur within the verse.  While the "weak" or "light" ending, where a single clause flows over, without any grammatical pause, from one verse to the next, becomes the most striking characteristic of his later metrical style.

Examples of "light endings" occur on every page; they are often of great beauty, and contribute to give the verse its largeness of contour:

> A lip of much contempt, speeds from me, and
> So leaves me, to consider (i. 2. 357).

Often the light ending is a single unstressed word following a strong pause:

> To bear the matter thus: mere weakness.  If (ii. 3. 2).

> I cannot be
> Mine own, nor any thing to any, if
> I be not thine (iv. 4. 43).

> Which does mend nature, change it rather, but
> The art itself is nature (iv. 4. 96).

### (iii) *Variations in Stress*

The greatest source of flexibility in Elizabethan verse lies in the endless modulations of stress. While quantity, in classical measures, is either short or long, stress may have an indefinite number of subtle gradations, and, provided that the five beats of the normal verse are sustained, or not overpowered, any degree of stress is admissible in any place. Thus, while the average verse has four main stresses, a verse made of a succession of monosyllables may have eight or nine, as in Milton's:

> Rocks, Caves, Lakes, Fens, Bogs, Dens, and shades of death
> (*Paradise Lost.* ii. 621).

And many verses of great beauty have three, or even two, e.g.

> Added to their familiárity (ii. 1. 167).
> So síngular in each partícular (iv. 4. 144).

Hence we find in the same foot all gradations from $(-'\ -')$ to $(x\ x)$, for the metrical beat either concurs with the stress or takes its place. Even the inversion $(- x)$ of the normal foot is not only admissible but of great beauty and constant occurrence, for the traversing of the normal rhythm, followed by its recovery, has the charm of a discord, in music, immediately resolved. Whereas a succession of five such feet would wholly change the character of the line, compelling us to refer it to another norm. Such a verse, indeed, we have in Lear's:

> Never, never, never, never, never!

But this is rather to be regarded as one of the countless dramatic departures from the norm than as a variation of it.

The possible variations in stress in a single Shakespearean verse are thus infinite, and could only be registered by a far finer notation than is at our disposal. It must suffice to give examples of the most marked and salient cases.

1. Feet without stress. Especially common at the end of the line:

> To me can life be no commodity (iii. 2. 90).

2. Feet with two stresses. This is often combined with 1, forming a figure of great beauty, particularly common in Milton. Its beauty arises from a momentary suspension of the normal time-measure, which is then immediately made good, as in the resolution of a discord in music:

> For the | flówers nów, | that frighted thou let'st fall (iv. 4. 117).
> Still betters what is done. When you | spéak, swéet (iv. 4. 136).

3. Feet with *inverted* stress. This also forms with a following normal foot a figure of great beauty. In the first foot this is common in all periods. In the fourth it is common in all periods of Shakespeare. It is less common in the third, rare in the second, very unusual in the fifth foot.

Occasionally it appears both in the second and fourth:

> So well, nothing so well; no, nor mean better (iv. 4. 374).

## 4. ABNORMAL VARIATIONS

But many verses are found, as already stated (iii. 2), in all Shakespeare's mature work, which cannot be referred to the norm at all. The general explanation being that dramatic truth has got the better of metrical fidelity, and to that extent deflected the verse from the norm. Almost all these verses occur where continuity is interrupted by a strong pause; especially by the division between two speeches.

1. The verse is abnormally long. We often find verses, normally of six feet, forming two phrases of three feet each.

(*a*) Within the same speech. Of this, though common in the more complex versification of the Tragedies, there seems to be no clear example in the present play. But it occurs occasionally without an internal pause:

> As you have ever been my father's honour'd friend (iv. 4. 486).

Also with a pause elsewhere than after the third foot:

> They say it is a copy out of mine. Come, captain (i. 2. 122).

(*b*) Between two speeches:

> The other for some while a friend.—Too hot, too hot! (i. 2. 108).
> Will you take eggs for money?—No, my lord, I'll fight (i. 2. 161).

2. The verse is abnormally short. Sometimes divided between two phrases:

> Two days ago. This jealousy (i. 2. 435).

(So, i. 2. 125).
Or between two speeches:

> *L.* You did mistake. *H.* No, if I mistake (ii. 1. 96).
> *P.* Should be "Remember mine". *L.* Stars, stars (v. 1. 67).

But also in a single phrase, usually one of heavily stressed syllables:

> Is goads, thorns, nettles, tails of wasps (i. 2. 313).

3. Often short lines, forming complete sentences, occur to mark a break or sudden turn in the thought, or an emphatic enforcement of it:

> Go to, go to! (i. 2. 182).

Even verses of a single foot:

> His smiles (ii. 3. 101).

Sometimes such short lines form a complete speech, introduced between complete verses:

> As merry as you will (ii. 1. 24).

It will be seen that this drama offers no parallel to the more violent dislocations of metre which in some of the crises of the Tragedies serve to mark intense excitement, as in the crucial dialogue of Othello with Desdemona (*Othello*, iii. 4. 80 *f.*). The emotional crises of *The Winter's Tale* are little less intense, but the men and women who suffer them are of less substance, their passions of less volume. To this less violent disturbance of the emotional temperature of the play, corresponds its more equable versification.

# GLOSSARY

affront (v. 1. 75), confront.

allow (iv. 1. 29), approve.

ancientry (iii. 3. 62), the elders, old people.

attach (v. 1. 182), arrest.

aunt (iv. 3. 11), "doxy".

bawcock (i. 2. 121), a term of endearment (*beau coq*).

blacks (i. 2. 132), mourning garments.

blank (ii. 3. 5), white centre of a target.

blench (i. 2. 317), swerve (from reason).

bug (iii. 2. 89), bugbear.

bugle (iv. 4. 217), bead of black glass.

caddis (iv. 4. 202), a worsted lace.

callat (ii. 3. 90), loose woman.

carbonado (iv. 4. 258), a broiled slice of meat.

centre (ii. 1. 98), the, the earth (as the centre of the planetary system). Cf. i. 2. 138, centre=*the inmost mind*.

character (iii. 3. 47), description (for identification).

cheat (iv. 3. 27), theft (see note).

child (iii. 3. 69), female infant.

childness (i. 2. 170), childish humours.

clamour (iv. 4. 241), constrain (a word of English origin, unconnected with its homonym).

clip (v. 2. 53), embrace.

commission (i. 2. 40), warrant.

commodity (iii. 2. 90), advantage.

conceit (iii. 2. 140), imagination.

condition (iv. 4. 708), nature.

credent (i. 2. 142), credible.

curst (iii. 3. 124), ill-tempered.

cypress (iv. 4. 214), crepe.

dildo (iv. 4. 194), a meaningless burden (in songs).

discovery (i. 2. 425), disclosure; cf. discover (ii. 1. 50).

disliken (iv. 4. 644), make unlike.

do (v. 2. 57, 98), express (of an artist).

doxy (iv. 3. 2), mistress.

149

**excrement** (iv. 4. 705), outgrowth, beard.

**fact** (iii. 2. 82), crime.
**fail** (ii. 3. 169; v. 1. 27), failure.
**fardel** (iv. 4. 699), bundle.
**farre** (iv. 4. 424), comp. farther.
**featly** (iv. 4. 176), daintily.
**fecks, i'** (i. 2. 120), in faith.
**federary** (ii. 1. 90), accomplice.
**fixure** (v. 3. 67), fixity.
**flap-dragon** (iii. 3. 94), swallow like a "flap-dragon"; see note.
**franklin** (v. 2. 157), yeoman.
**free** (ii. 3. 30), innocent; **(iv. 4. 542)**, willing.

**gest** (i. 2. 41), an appointed stage in a journey, especially in a royal progress.
**gillyvor** (iv. 4. 82), "gillyflowers".
**gossip** (ii. 3. 41), sponsor.

**hand-fast** (iv. 4. 760), custody.
**harlot** (ii. 3. 4), rascal (masculine).
**having** (iv. 4. 710), property.
**heft** (ii. 1. 45), retching.
**hox** (i. 2. 230), hamstring, maim.

**immodest** (iii. 2. 99), immoderate.
**importance** (v. 2. 18), import.
**industriously** (i. 2. 242), deliberately.
**inkle** (iv. 4. 202), a tape.
**instance** (iv. 4. 587), proof.

**intelligent** (i. 2. 362), communication.

**jar** (i. 2. 43), tick.

**knack** (iv. 4. 342, 421), plaything, trinket.

**land-damn** (ii. 1. 139), (probably) abuse.  See note.
**level** (ii. 3. 6), range.
**limber** (i. 2. 47), pliant.
**lozel** (ii. 3. 108), rogue.
**lunes** (ii. 2. 30), capricious moods.

**mankind** (ii. 3. 67), *adj.* masterful.
**means** (iv. 3. 42), tenors.
**methoughts** (i. 2. 154), for "methought" on the analogy of "methinks".
**mort** (i. 2. 118), in hunting, notes of the horn, announcing the death of the quarry.
**motion** (iv. 3. 93), puppet-show.

**neat** (i. 2. 125), cattle.
**neb** (i. 2. 183), bill, lips.
**note** (i. 1. 35), observation.
— (i. 2. 2), reckoning.

**overture** (ii. 1. 164), disclosure.

**pantler** (iv. 4. 56), pantry attendant.
**pash** (i. 2. 128), head, forehead.
**perfect** (iii. 3. 1), assured.
**piece** (iv. 4. 32, 415), excellent example, paragon; (v. 2. 105), *v.* piece out, complete.
**pin (and web)** (i. 2. 274), cataract.

**pinch** (ii. 1. 51), trick, out-wit.

**plackets** (iv. 4. 237), stom-achers.

**points** (iv. 4. 200), tagged laces (with a pun, see note).

**poking-sticks** (iv. 4. 221), rods used in starching the frills of ruffs.

**practice** (iii. 2. 163), knavery.

**proper** (ii. 3. 139), own, *adj*.

**preposterous** (v. 2. 144), the clown's blunder for "pros-perous".

**present** (i. 2. 264), instant, immediate.

**pretence** (iii. 2. 16), design.

**prig** (iv. 3. 98), thief.

**professor** (v. 1. 108), one who "professes" a creed.

**purchase** (iv. 4. 504), procure, win.

**question** (v. 1. 198), exam-ination (by torture).

**rash** (i. 2. 302), quick.

**rehearse** (v. 2. 61), repeat.

**remember** (iii. 2. 226), re-mind.

**replenish'd** (ii. 1. 79), com-plete.

**round** (i. 2. 203), whisper.

**sad** (iv. 4. 303), serious.

**saltier** (iv. 4. 319), satyr (a rustic version of the word).

**scape** (iii. 3. 70), slip, fault.

**singular** (iv. 4. 144), unique.

**skill** (iv. 4. 152), reason.

**sleeve-hand** (iv. 4. 204), wristband.

**sneaping** (i. 2. 13), nipping.

**square** (iv. 4. 205), a part of the female dress covering the breast.

**squash** (i. 2. 160), unripe peapod.

**squier** (iv. 4. 332), foot-rule.

**stuff'd** (ii. 1. 177), sufficient.

**success** (i. 2. 378), succes-sion.

**tall** (v. 2. 161), active, able.

**tawdry-lace** (iv. 4. 243), a neat handkerchief or lace.

**tempt** (ii. 2. 50), solicit.

**toaze** (iv. 4. 726), touse, pluck.

**troll-my-dames** (iv. 3. 85), a game; see note.

**undergo** (ii. 3. 163), under-take.

**unrolled** (iv. 3. 119), struck off the roll (of thieves).

**vast** (i. 1. 29), boundless sea.

**vice** (i. 2. 400), force.

**virginaling** (i. 2. 125), play-ing as on a virginal or spin-net.

**ward** (i. 2. 33), posture (in fencing).

**welkin** (i. 2. 136), sky.

**whoo-bub** (iv. 4. 608), hub-bub.

**wink** (i. 2. 300), close the eyes, sleep.

**woman-tired** (ii. 3. 74), "hen-pecked".

**yest** (iii. 3. 90), foam.

# INDEX

"not", its position in the sentence, iv. 4. 464.

old tale, v. 2. 60; v. 3. 117.

*Pandosto*, iv. 1. *ad init.* See also *Greene, Robert.*
paronomasia, ii. 3. 49; iv. 4. 200, 805.
picking the teeth, iv. 4. 745.
pin and web, i. 2. 274.
poking-stick, iv. 4. 221.
posts, iii. 2. 98.
pugging, iv. 3. 8.
puppet-shows, iv. 3. 93.
puritans, iv. 3. 42.

recognition-scene, v. 2. *ad init.*; v. 3. *ad init.*

*Reynard the Fox*, ii. 3. 75.
"romances", characteristics of, i. 2. *ad init.*; ii. 1. *ad init.*; ii. 2. *ad init.*; ii. 3. *ad init.*; iii. 1. 21; iii. 2. *ad init.*, 119, 142; iii. 3. *ad init.*, 56; iv. 4. *ad init.*; v. 2. 95; v. 3. *ad init.*

scansion, i. 2. 313; v. 3. 52.
sneaping, i. 2. 13.
spider, supposed venomous, ii. i. 39.

through, thorough, iii. 2. 167.
tods, iv. 3. 31.
troll-my dames, iv. 3. 85.

vast, i. 1. 29.

# SHAKESPEARE'S STAGE IN ITS BEARING
# UPON HIS DRAMA

§ 1. The structure and arrangements of the Elizabethan theatre are still under discussion, and many points of detail remain unsettled. A very extensive and highly technical literature on the subject is available, chiefly in England, America, and Germany. It is based especially on the new evidence derived from (1) the original stage directions, (2) contemporary illustrations and descriptions. The following summary gives the conclusions which at present appear most reasonable, neglecting much speculative matter of great interest.

§ 2. When Shakespeare arrived in London, soon after 1585, theatrical exhibitions were given there in (1) public theatres, (2) private theatres, (3) the halls of the royal palaces, and of the Inns of Court.

Of the ' public ' theatres there were at least three: The Theater, the Curtain, both in Shoreditch, and Newington Butts on the Bankside or Southwark shore. About 1587, the Rose, also on the Bankside, was added. All these were occasionally used by Shakespeare's company before 1599, when their headquarters became the newly built Globe, likewise on the Bankside. Of the ' private ' theatres the principal, and the oldest, was the Blackfriar, on the site of the present *Times* office. It was also the property of the company in which Shakespeare acquired a share, but being let out practically his whole career, does not count in the present connexion. At court, on the other hand, his company played repeatedly. But his plays were written for the ' public ' theatre, and this alone had any influence in his stage-craft.

§ 3. The ' public ' theatre differed from the other two types chiefly in being (1) dependent on daylight, (2) open overhead, and (3) partially seatless; and from the court-stages also, in (4) not using painted scenes. While they, again, had the rectangular form, the typical ' public ' theatre was a round or octagonal edifice, modelled partly on the inn-yards where companies of players had been accustomed to perform, prior to the inhibition of 1574, on movable stages; partly on the arenas used for bear-baiting and cock-fighting;—sports still carried on in the ' theatres ', and in part dictating their arrangements.

The circular inner area, known thence as the ' cock-pit ', or ' pit ', had accordingly no seats; admission to it cost one penny (6*d*. in modern money), and the throng of standing spectators were known as the ' groundlings '. More expensive places (up to 2*s*. 6*d*.) with seats, were provided in tiers of galleries which ran round the area, one above the other, as in modern theatres; the uppermost being covered with a thatched roof.

§ 4. **The Stage** (using the term to describe the entire scenic apparatus of the theatre) included (1) the *outer stage*, a rectangular platform (as much as 42 feet wide in the largest examples) projecting into the circular area, from the back wall, and thus surrounded by ' groundlings ' on three sides. Above it were a thatched roof and hangings but no side or front curtains. In the floor was a trap-door by which ghosts and others ascended or descended. At the back were (2) two projecting wings, each with a door opening obliquely on to the stage, the *recess* between them, of uncertain shape and extent, forming a kind of inner stage. Above this was (3) an upper room or rooms, which included the actors' ' tiring house ', with a window or

windows opening on to (4) a *balcony* or gallery from which was hung
(5) a *curtain*, by means of which the inner recess could be concealed or
disclosed.

§ 5. The most important divergence of this type of structure from
that of our theatres is in the relation between the outer stage and the
auditorium. In the modern theatre the play is treated as a picture,
framed in the proscenium arch, seen by the audience like any other
picture from the front only, and shut off from their view at any
desired moment by letting fall the curtain. An immediate consequence of this was that a scene (or act) could terminate only in one
of two ways. Either the persons concerned in it walked, or were
carried, off the stage; or a change of place and circumstances was
*supposed* without their leaving it. Both these methods were used.
The first was necessary only at the close of the play. For this reason
an Elizabethan play rarely ends on a *climax* such as the close of
Ibsen's *Ghosts*; the overpowering effect of which would be gravely
diminished if, instead of the curtain falling upon Osvald's helpless
cry for "the sun", he and his mother had to walk off the stage.
Marlowe's *Faustus* ends with a real climax, because the catastrophe
*ipso facto* leaves the stage clear. But the close of even the most over-
whelming final scenes of Shakespeare is relatively quiet, or even, as
in *Macbeth*, a little tame. The concluding lines often provide a motive
for the (compulsory) clearing of the stage.

In the *Tragedies*, the dead body of the hero has usually to be borne ceremoniously
away, followed by the rest; so Aufidius in *Coriolanus*: "Help, three o' the chiefest
soldiers: I'll be one". Similarly in *Hamlet* and *King Lear*. In *Othello*, Desdemona's bed was apparently in the curtained recess, and at the close the curtains
were drawn upon the two bodies, instead of their being as usual borne away.

The close of the *Histories* often resembles the dispersing of an informal council
after a declaration of policy by the principal person; thus *Richard II.* closes with
Bolingbroke's announcement of the penance he proposes to pay for Richard's
death; *Henry IV.* with his orders for the campaign against Northumberland and
Glendower; *King John* with Falconbridge's great assertion of English patriotism.

In the *Comedies*, the leading persons will often withdraw to explain to one
another at leisure what the audience already knows (*Winter's Tale, Tempest,
Merchant of Venice*), or to carry out the wedding rites (*As You Like It, Midsummer-
Night's Dream*); or they strike up a measure and thus (as in *Much Ado*) naturally
dance off the stage. Sometimes the chief persons have withdrawn before the close,
leaving some minor character—Puck (*Midsummer-Night's Dream*) or the Clown
(*Twelfth Night*)—to wind up the whole with a snatch of song, and then retire
himself.

§ 6. But the most important result of the exposed stage was that it
placed strict limit upon dramatic illusion, and thus compelled the
resort, for most purposes, to conventions resting on symbolism, suggestion, or make-believe. It was only in dress that anything like
simulation could be attempted; and here the Elizabethan companies,
as is well known, were lavish in the extreme. Painted scenes, on the
other hand, even had they been available, would have been idle or
worse, when perhaps a third of the audience would see, behind the
actors, not the scenes but the people in the opposite gallery, or the
gallants seated on the stage. Especially where complex and crowded
actions were introduced, the most beggarly symbolic suggestion was
cheerfully accepted. Jonson, in the spirit of classical realism, would